AGELESS ATH

SWIMMING
Past 50

Mel Goldstein
Past President, United States Masters Swimming

Dave Tanner
Indiana University Human Performance Lab

Human Kinetics

D0043606

Library of Congress Cataloging-in-Publication Data

Goldstein, Mel, 1938-
  Swimming past 50 / Mel Goldstein and Dave Tanner.
    p. cm. -- (Ageless athlete series)
  Includes bibliographical references (p.) and index.
  ISBN 0-88011-907-1
  1. Swimming for the aged. I. Tanner, Dave, 1950- . II. Title.
  III. Title: Swimming past fifty. IV. Series.
  GV837.3.G65 1999
  797.2'1' 0846--dc21   99-12569
                                                                          CIP

ISBN: 0-88011-907-1

Developmental Editors: Syd Slobodnik and Joanna Hatzopoulos; **Assistant Editors:** Kim Thoren, Henry Woolsey, and Pamela S. Johnson; **Copyeditor:** Don Ammerman; **Indexer:** Sharon Duffy; **Graphic Designer:** Robert Reuther; **Graphic Artist:** Tara Welsch; **Photo Editor:** Clark Brooks; **Cover Designer:** Keith Blomberg; **Photographer (cover):** W. D. Smith of Photo Smiths; **Photographer (interior):** All photographs by Michael Lindsay unless otherwise noted; **Illustrator**: Chuck Nivens; **Printer:** United Graphics

Human Kinetics books are available at special discounts for bulk purchase. Special editions or book excerpts can also be created to specification. For details, contact the Special Sales Manager at Human Kinetics.

Printed in the United States of America   10 9 8 7 6 5 4 3 2 1

Human Kinetics
Web site: http: // www.humankinetics.com/

United States: Human Kinetics, P.O. Box 5076, Champaign, IL 61825-5076
1-800-747-4457
e-mail: humank@hkusa.com

Canada: Human Kinetics, 475 Devonshire Road Unit 100, Windsor, ON N8Y 2L5
1-800-465-7301 (in Canada only)
e-mail: humank@hkcanada.com

Europe: Human Kinetics, P.O. Box IW14, Leeds LS16 6TR, United Kingdom
+44 (0)113-278 1708
e-mail: humank@hkeurope.com

Australia: Human Kinetics, 57A Price Avenue, Lower Mitcham, South Australia 5062
(08) 82771555
e-mail: humank@hkaustralia.com

New Zealand: Human Kinetics, P.O. Box 105-231, Auckland Central
09-523-3462
e-mail: humank@hknewz.com

Dedicated to Doc and Marge Counsilman

Doc
Our Coach, Teacher, Mentor, and Friend

Marge
The inspiration for this book

Contents

Preface

Swimming is the ideal activity for lifetime fitness. *Swimming Past 50* is intended to address the concerns of the serious swimmer over 50 years of age. The physiological benefits of regular exercise as a means of slowing the aging process are well documented, but there are emotional benefits as well. Because swimming is such a technical sport, the potential for improvement in performance is tremendous, even for swimmers in their 80s or 90s. At a time in life when most physical capabilities are in decline, it is especially gratifying to see improvement in a physical activity. In our years of teaching and coaching swimmers over the age of 50 we've been constantly amazed at the enthusiasm, willingness to learn, and stellar performances achieved by people who picked up the sport later in life. For us, sharing their joy is the most rewarding aspect of our job as teacher and coach.

Swimming Past 50 is not a "learn to swim" book. There are already several technical books on the market that cover the intricacies of stroke technique in great detail, including one directed specifically toward the older adult, *Swimming for Seniors* by Edward Shea, also published by Human Kinetics. Dr. Shea, holder of several national records in the 80-84 age group, presents an excellent introduction to swimming for the older adult who wishes to use the sport as a fitness activity. *Swimming Past 50* adds to the material in *Swimming for Seniors* and covers in more depth the benefits of an intense, structured training program, in order to prepare for competition. We also address issues relevant to the past-50 swimmer that may not appear in books aimed at younger audiences.

What is the potential of the past-50 swimmer? Can a 50-, 70-, or 90- year-old really train hard, achieve top performances, and continue to enjoy swimming? Real-life examples aren't hard to find. We asked eight over-50 swimmers to tell us about their training programs and what swimming means to them. Although most of them participated in some form of competitive swimming in their youth, many were not particularly serious about it. They're certainly not ordinary people today! They hold numerous world and national records in their respective age groups. Their comments echo many of the sentiments expressed in this book. A common thread runs through all of their stories: they work out very hard! Furthermore, they show no signs of intending to back off any time soon. They've chosen to make competitive swimming a lifelong activity. All of them train with other people, either informally or as part of a team with a coach. In fact, getting together with friends, both within and outside the competitive arena, is a major factor in their motivation to continue swimming. Gold medals and world records aren't necessary in order to benefit from the sport.

It's never too late to enjoy fulfillment and recognition for your athletic achievements. There are millions of people over the age of 50 who use swimming as a means of maintaining fitness. We hope that this book will help you to increase your enjoyment of our beloved sport.

Acknowledgments

We would like to thank Walter Gantz, PhD, past-50 runner-turned-swimmer, for his enthusiastic assistance during the development of this manuscript. Walt is the type of athlete for whom this book was intended, so we structured the content according to what he wanted to know about swimming. He made so many valuable suggestions and did so much proof-reading of the manuscript that he should be listed as the third author! Stephanie Janssen, PT/ATC, head athletic trainer for aquatic sports at Indiana University and specialist in aquatic physical therapy, made valuable contributions to the sections covering prevention and treatment of swimming injuries. Ada Pennington of the Indiana University HPER library gave valuable research assistance. Swimming photographs were taken at the Indiana University pools in Bloomington and Indianapolis. We would like to thank Joanna Hatzopoulos at Human Kinetics for her contributions as an editor. We gratefully acknowledge the contribution made by our fellow Masters swimmers who shared their experiences with and love for the sport. And finally, we thank Doc and Marge Counsilman, who guided us along the path of a lifetime devotion to the sport of swimming. Doc gave us more than the love for a sport. While we were members of his swim team at Indiana, and throughout the years since, his words and actions taught us to believe in ourselves, to work hard at reaching the potential he saw in us. We hope that in some small way this book will serve as a tribute to all that he means to us.

chapter 1

Swimming: Exercise for a Lifetime

Swimming is the perfect exercise for lifetime fitness. No other activity provides so many health benefits with so few dangers. The older athlete is especially concerned about staying healthy because consistency is essential for a fitness program to be effective, and avoiding injury is the key to consistency. Water is a wonderfully *forgiving* medium. Gone is the jarring of running. Absent are the dangers of cycling. Dogs, cars, angry people, potholes, curbs, inclement weather, and even air pollution are potential injury-causing factors that can be avoided in the environment most often encountered by the fitness swimmer. The swimming pool is a safe environment by design. Although no one expects to need it, emergency assistance from a lifeguard is usually available and never more than a few seconds away, a service that gives comfort to individuals with health problems who may not have the confidence to attempt an exercise program otherwise.

Besides emergency assistance, swimming in a pool offers many advantages over other modes of exercise. Unlike running and cycling, if you get tired in the middle of a workout, you are only a few feet from the end of the pool instead of being miles from home. When you run out of gas, the workout is over and you get out. This allows you to safely test your limits, to extend your usual range of distance or time. Scheduling your daily exercise time is more rigid for swimming than it is for biking, running, or weight lifting. This can be viewed as an advantage or a disadvantage. Although you can exercise outdoors by running or cycling at almost any hour of the day, most pools don't offer unlimited lap swimming times. You must schedule your workout to fit the hours the pool is open. Because most people over the age of 50 lead busy lives, a rigid schedule is often a blessing. When exercise time is an option, it's too easy to put it off until later in the day, too easy to put it off entirely. When swim practice is scheduled at a specific time, and you will miss your swim if you do not go at that time, you tend to force yourself to go even on those days when it would be easier to skip. Remember, the key to a successful exercise program is consistency, and a planned schedule promotes consistency. Finally, swimming is a social sport. You've heard about the loneliness of the long-distance runner and cycling down a lonesome country road, but there are very few lonely swimmers. Certainly you spend most of your workout with your face in the water, but this only serves as valuable thinking time for future discussions with your training partners during rest intervals.

Old Isn't What It Used to Be

When organized Masters swimming competition began in 1970, the oldest age group was 45 and over. Now, after almost 30 years of growth, it's 100 and over! Even a 100-year-old person is not too old to compete in swimming. As life expectancy continues to increase, our definition of "old" has changed. In today's terminology, "middle age" starts at 45 and lasts until age 64. At 65 we become "young-old" and don't advance to "old" until we reach 75. The age span from 85 to 99 is termed "old-old," and if you're lucky enough to live past 100 you're one of the "oldest-old."

Physical activity plays a role in enhancing the quality of life throughout all of these stages. In middle age, regular exercise can improve self-esteem and maintain physical function. In those over 65, exercise improves mobility and serves as a means to stimulate social interaction. In those over 85, exercise can make the difference between independent living and helplessness. The medical profession now is promoting exercise as the best way to minimize the debilitating effects of old age, and the mode of exercise most often recommended is swimming. No matter what stage of aging you may be in now, if you look to the future and take care of yourself by exercising regularly, you can enjoy the benefits of a healthier life. Ultimately, you are only as old as you want to be!

Exercise Is a Choice

In today's world, exercise is a lifestyle choice. The physical strength and endurance so necessary to our ancestors in their struggle against the environment are no longer qualities that are paramount to our survival. We have buildings to protect us and machines to do our work. We can live a totally sedentary life and never have to worry about the source of our next meal, as long as we can get to the grocery store before it closes!

These fitness swimmers enjoy the benefits of regular exercise.

Let's consider, for a moment, the life cycle of animals living in the natural world. In general, newborn animals are physically active in play and competition with their littermates. In their youth they train to acquire the stamina and skills needed to survive as adults. During their reproductive years they need to be strong and healthy to attract a mate and provide food for their family. As aging progresses, it's normal for animals to become less and less physically active; their bodies degenerate to the point of being consumed by disease or a faster animal.

Normal human biology follows a life cycle pattern similar to that of animals. Many older adults, however, choose to be "abnormal" by remaining physically active throughout their lives, by refusing to yield to the degeneration associated with growing old. There are many reasons why they make this choice, the primary ones being to maintain good health and feel good about themselves. But as opportunities for swimming competition in the older age groups have increased over the last 30 years, the desire to be physically fit has grown as well.

Physical fitness is defined as living up to your physiological potential, living your life fully with quality. In our youth we may not have appreciated our fitness, thinking it would last forever, but now that we can feel the effects of aging, we're more aware of what we're losing. We sense our mortality. We have less strength, less endurance, and less mobility. For each of us who enjoys physical challenges, it can be very depressing to feel physical capabilities decreasing year by year. We choose to exercise because being physically strong makes us feel better about ourselves. There are so many changes associated with aging over which we have no control—changes in hair color, hair loss, wrinkles—that it's refreshing to be able to take command of at least one aspect of our lives, our level of physical fitness.

"You should spend at least two hours a day on bodily exercise. However, if you should decide not to, you will someday spend two hours a day taking care of your disease." This sounds like a very modern statement, but these thoughts actually were expressed by Thomas Jefferson. How prophetic his words were, based on what we know today about the benefits of exercise and the maintenance of health as we age. Certainly his concept of exercise didn't include swimming laps in a pool or pushing weights in the gym. His bodily exercise probably consisted of walking, riding a horse, or chopping wood, all excellent forms of exercise. Today, of course, we have a much greater variety of options. All we need is the desire to sample.

Despite the overwhelming evidence in support of regular physical activity as a means of maintaining health into old age, most older adults choose to be "normal" and not exercise. Approximately 55 percent of the U.S. adult population is sedentary, totally inactive, not even bowling once a year. The percentage of people who train regularly has been estimated to be between 15 and 20 percent. Clearly the older adult who swims regularly is "abnormal" compared with the general population in the United States. The good news is swimming is one of our country's most popular participant sports, possibly because it is recognized as the ideal exercise to carry us through the aging process. Swimming is the best choice for many reasons. It's a sport that involves the entire body, without placing too much stress on any part of it. It can be a clean, highly structured sport, with numerous opportunities for competition in a relaxed, socially pleasant environment. But most importantly, it's a sport we can continue to enjoy as we age. Many elderly swimmers have stated they won't stop swimming until the day they die. As Masters swimmer Graham Johnston says, "I hope to die in the pool and be the healthiest corpse in the cemetery!"

Exercise, Aging, and Performance

Is it really possible to slow down the aging process? Scientific studies conducted with both humans and animals can give us some answers to that question. Scientists don't like to go out on a limb, but they are fairly certain that persons who are more physically active live longer than those who are sedentary. Put another way, a consistent exercise program increases life expectancy. For those who don't want to exercise, animal studies have demonstrated another means of increasing life expectancy, but it definitely would not be an option for those who enjoy eating. One controversial study found that rats fed two-thirds of a normal rat diet lived longer than rats that ate as much as they wanted. This finding has not been promoted widely because the longevity benefits of food restriction have not been confirmed in humans. Besides, do you really want to give up eating?

There's no controversy, however, about the benefits of exercise in *slowing* the aging process. It comes as no surprise that the old saying, "use it or lose it," applies to the physical components of the body. If aging can be viewed as a diminution in physical capacity, then anything we can do to prevent "losing it" should diminish the rate of aging. Such has been shown to be the case. In fact, the ability of the aged human body to adapt to training has been a pleasant surprise to many exercise scientists. Even subjects in their 90s respond to training in much the same manner, with all the same adaptations, as seen in teenagers. The ability of the older adult to adapt to training is especially evident in swimming. There are a few 60- and 70-year-olds who can still give the high schoolers a run for their money in the pool! Your body is ready to be trained! Are you?

Doc Counsilman, a legendary past-50 swimmer, demonstrates proper technique to his students.

Courtesy of IU Athletic Media Relations

The reason some 70-year-old swimmers can outperform teenagers is because swimming is such a technical sport. Proper stroke mechanics and efficiency can compensate for the superior strength and endurance of youth. This makes swimming the ideal sport for the older athlete who wants to enjoy the thrills of improvement in a physical activity. Past the age of 50, the well-trained athlete is at a physical stage where further training will not produce a big change in performance. Improved technique, however, will extract every bit of physical potential that's available. We've seen numerous swimmers who have been able to match performances from their youth through a combination of careful training and better stroke mechanics. The results for swimmers who pick up the sport late in life are even more dramatic. As they learn how to swim more efficiently, they do lifetime bests every time they dive into the pool. It's a great feeling for them, and their coaches, too!

Of course swimming isn't going to transform someone from the "old-old" age group into a teenager. But, it can certainly help the 90-year-old live a fuller life. There are some losses of physical capacity over which we have no control. Nevertheless,

© 1995 Terry Wild Studio

Swimming can preserve your youthful spirit.

there are many more that readily respond to increased use by becoming stronger, more resilient, and more youthful in function. We have to take the bad with the good and be glad we can win at least some of the battles against aging, even if we eventually will lose the war. It's essential that we never give up. We may have to make a few compromises along the way, but we must never capitulate.

Fitness Swimming

Someone who uses swimming as a fitness activity can be called a "fitness swimmer." It's impossible to estimate how many of the approximately 70 million people in the United States who claim to participate in swimming as a recreational activity actually swim for fitness (as opposed to spending the day at the beach) nor do we know the percentage of fitness swimmers over the age of 50. We do know, however, how many older fitness swimmers compete. The national organization for adult competitive swimming in the U.S. is the United States Masters Swimming (USMS). In 1997, the USMS registry listed 32,119 swimmers, ranging in age from 19 to 99. The breakdown of the number in each of the 50 and over age groups is displayed in table 1.1. The 7,603 past-50 swimmers account for about 24% of the USMS total, but they are a small fraction of the people past 50 who swim for fitness.

A rough estimate of the number of past-50 fitness swimmers is probably between 2 and 3 million people in the United States alone. That's a lot of people, and the numbers will continue to increase as the "baby boom" generation moves into the older age groups. This generation grew up during the 1950s at a time when participation in age group swimming for children exploded, so there's a huge wave of experienced swimmers joining the ranks of the past-50 club. It's only been since World War II that sport for the masses has really blossomed. The baby boomers grew up bombarded by competitive sports programs and are convinced of the importance of exercise for improving quality of life. As these people retire, and/or wake up to their own mortality, we are going to see a "swimmer boom" of gray-haired athletes in pools all across the country.

Table 1.1

NUMBER OF USMS REGISTERED SWIMMERS BY AGE GROUP, 1997

Age Group	Combined	Women	Men
50–54	2,759	893	1,866
55–59	1,520	518	1,002
60–64	1,056	400	656
65–69	859	327	532
70–74	676	265	411
75–79	393	157	236
80–84	242	76	166
85–89	85	36	49
90–94	12	4	8
95–99	1	1	0
100+	0	0	0
Total	7,603	2,677	4,926

More people than ever will reap the benefits of swimming for fitness. It will be glorious!

Structured Training

To most people, swimming for fitness means going to the pool, completing a predetermined number of laps at a steady pace, and going home. The goal is to burn calories. Performance is not an issue. Swimming is a recreational activity, an activity to be enjoyed for the simple pleasures of being in the water. Done consistently, fitness swimming can be sufficient to maintain reasonable health. As mentioned before, anyone who exercises regularly is part of the minority in our society that is concerned about fitness.

But there are those who aren't satisfied with swimming just to burn calories. As human beings we're competitive and goal-oriented by nature. We like to compete against others, against our past performances, and against our own potential. We might even include aging as our fiercest competitor, a foe to

Competition can be fun at any age!

which we refuse to yield. The next step toward improved performance against our competitors, especially aging, is the structured workout. Adding structure to a fitness swimming program transforms *lap swimming* into a *workout*. Structure adds variety and challenge to a training program, factors that improve motivation. The next step after the structured workout is the group training session, either informally with a group of friends or as a member of a team. With team membership come the benefits of professional coaching, so essential for improving stroke mechanics. Structured workouts, a group of friends, a team, a coach—it sounds just like the age group swimming programs that were so popular with our children. The beauty of Masters swimming is that it promotes a youthful attitude, almost as if we were kids again.

Of course we aren't kids again. A 50-year-old athlete cannot be expected to follow the same training regimen as a 20-year-old college student. Neither can a 90-year-old train like a 50-year-old. We must know our limits. Physically we're not the same people we were 30, 40, or 50 years ago, and we'd be inviting injury to train as if we were. The workout structure for the 90-year-old swimmer should be different from that designed for the 50-year-old—less distance, more rest, fewer repeats, and less intensity. We'll discuss the details of workout structure in chapters 3 and 4.

Competitive Swimming

The next logical step for some swimmers who have adopted a structured approach to their training is to enter organized competitions. For others daily workouts against the clock are satisfying enough and serve as motivation to swim regularly. Competition can take the form of meets held in a pool, or triathlons, or open water swims. We would like to emphasize, however, that competing is not a requirement for reaping the benefits of a structured training program. The structure *is* essential. Without structure, it's more difficult to focus your energies so as to maximize improvements in performance. The benefits to be gained by improving technique, by doing organized workouts, and by training with a group are still attainable without swimming in a meet. Competition merely serves as a valuable motivational tool. For the Masters swimmer,

Mary E. Messenger

Competition turns exercise into a social event.

GRAHAM JOHNSTON

Home: Houston, Texas
Current age group: 65 to 69
Started Masters swimming at age 40

Graham learned to swim at age one, began competing at age six, and continued in the sport throughout his school years, including four years at the University of Oklahoma. The highlight of his early swimming career was participation in the 1952 Olympics in Helsinki. Other sports he enjoyed include soccer, rugby, field hockey, tennis, gymnastics, diving, water polo, and rowing. His career as a Masters swimmer is even more impressive, so much so that in 1998 he was elected to the International Swimming Hall of Fame, an accomplishment that is more significant to him than swimming in the Olympics. He has been especially successful in recent years, winning 11 gold medals in the Tokyo (1986) and Montreal (1994) world championship meets and setting 45 world records in the past six years. He currently owns 41 world records, 31 world championship titles, 100 national records, and 87 national championship titles. As an example of what a 66-year-old can do, in 1997 he swam 1:05.09 for 100 meters, 10:29.26 for 800 meters, 20:04.73 for 1,500 meters, and broke the national record for 6,000 yards by over 17 minutes.

Courtesy of Graham Johnston

Graham is also an open water specialist. He was the first 60–64 year-old to break one hour in the Waikiki Rough Water Swim (51:45) and at age 64 was the oldest and fastest ever to swim from Robben Island to Cape Town (10 km in 51-degree water). The following year he placed 13th out of 400 entrants of all ages in the Alcatraz to San Francisco swim. Of course, he won the 65-69 age group! In 1998 he had an especially busy schedule, competing in four open water races (Santa Cruz, Donner Lake, La Jolla, and Waikiki) that ranged in distance from three to six miles.

Graham doesn't have a coach, but he has been training with Bill Cerny for the past 25 years. Bill usually makes up the workouts, which are often longer than Graham would like to go. He doesn't lift weights for fear of injury. He swims for health because it makes him feel mentally alert and physically fit, plus he tends to eat and sleep well when he swims. His wife Janis supports him 100 percent. They like to travel to meets to see new places and meet up with their Masters friends.

Graham's Sample Workout
(10 days prior to Long Course Nationals):

Warm-up: 500 Swim, 500 Kick, 500 Pull

Swim 10 × 100 meters on 1:40

Swim 10 × 100 meters on 1:35

Swim 10 × 100 meters on 1:30

   (Rest 1:00 between sets)

competition is usually not an end in itself, as it often is for the Olympic competitor. The result of this more relaxed attitude about competition is that there is a tremendously important social aspect to adult competitive swimming. What we often see is a group of fun-loving people enjoying the company of others their own age. It is a fortuitous bonus that the activity around which this social interaction takes place is a healthy one.

The authors are very excited about the potential of the past-50 swimmer. Nobody likes to get older, but swimming, of all the physical activities available to you, offers the best opportunity for satisfaction as the years pass by. With age comes wisdom. Over and over again we have observed how the positive aspects of being wiser can be combined with the negative aspects of being older into an exercise plan that promotes health and happiness in one's life. We're constantly impressed by the enthusiasm of the past-50 swimmers we have coached and taught. Almost without exception, they are like sponges, eager to soak up new information about swimming—new training methods, new stroke techniques, new equipment, anything they can use to improve their performance. They're enthused about swimming because they can *see* improvements in their performance from year to year, despite the effects of aging, and they look forward to their future in the sport.

In writing this book we, as authors, were challenged by the fact that our potential audience is so diverse. Our readers range in age by as much as 50 years and have different physical capacities, skill levels, goals, and motivation. It would be impossible to address in great detail the special needs of the middle-age, the young-old, the old, the old-old, and the oldest-old athlete, male and female, in a book of this size. Instead, we've presented the basics of swim training, with general advice for the past-50 athlete. When trying to adapt structured training methods to your own individual physical and mental situation, the best specific advice we can give is the following: *Stay within your capabilities!* Do not try to do more than you can handle. Only you know your true limits, and only you can decide if our recommendations are within them. It may be necessary to modify the quantity and quality of our workout examples to fit within your capabilities. It may be necessary to swim fewer yards and take longer rest intervals. Ideally, a coach who is familiar with your skills would make these changes for you. The important aspect of adding structure to training is for you to reach your potential as a swimmer, even without a coach on the deck. We believe you can do it!

Many of the recommendations in this book involve strenuous physical activity. Consult your physician before attempting to increase the intensity or duration of your normal exercise routine.

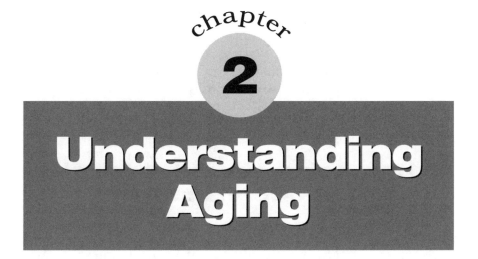

chapter 2

Understanding Aging

The relationship between aging and performance is a "bad news–good news" scenario. The bad news is that performance declines with age. Estimates place the decline at about 1 percent per year after the age of 25. The good news is that exercise can slow down the aging process and, hence, the decline in performance. For many years it was believed aging was inevitable, that the latter years of life would have to be reserved for sedentary activities. Intense exercise was considered dangerous. Fortunately, this belief is changing, due in part to the outstanding physical performances by Masters swimmers in recent years. As we shall see, scientific research supports the anecdotal evidence that we have more control over the aging process than previously believed. To some extent, aging appears to be more a result of a sedentary lifestyle than an inevitable decline in physical capacity. The early promoters of lifelong fitness were right: exercise can improve the quality of life at any age.

Obviously there are some aspects of aging over which we have no control, such as physical changes that are determined by genetics. People age at different rates. The genetically lucky individuals are those who are capable of exercising vigorously as they age. In swimming, the method of grouping competitors by age is not always fair. In youth group swimming, the early maturers have an advantage. In Masters swimming, the late agers have the advantage. The disparity between early and late agers becomes more noticeable in the over-50 age groups. Comparing yourself with a person who is genetically gifted with slow aging can be discouraging. When setting reasonable performance goals for yourself it may be wise to gauge your progress against your own efforts over the past couple of years rather than using the standard set by others.

How Aging Affects Physical Performance

Masters swimming is the ideal laboratory for the study of aging and performance. Since its inception in 1970, membership has grown into the tens of thousands in this country and throughout the world. Each year championship meets are held, with as many as 2,300 participants. Researchers have used the times recorded in these meets to plot the effects of aging on performance. A study conducted in 1975, in the early days of Masters swimming, confirmed the 1 percent per year decline observed in other aging studies. But a more recent study conducted in 1992 by Phil Whitten found Masters swimmers do not begin to decline until their mid-30s, and the annual rate does not reach 1 percent until their 70s! Compare these results with what would be predicted from the traditional 1 percent per year decline. Living a sedentary lifestyle, by age 50 your physical capacity will have declined by 23 percent from what it was at age 25. By age 75 your capacity will be only 40 percent. But the Masters swimmers studied declined only 3.5 percent by age 50 and only 19.1 percent by age 75. Masters swimming is leading the way in demonstrating the benefits of exercise in slowing the aging process.

When discussing the effects of aging on physical performance, it's very difficult to distinguish between the effects of aging *per se* and those due to a sedentary lifestyle. If we go to the pool and stand a 20-year-old college swimmer next to a 60-year-old Masters swimmer, we can see obvious differences because we are comparing individuals from distinct sections of the population of swimmers. We call this a cross-sectional comparison. Due to individual differences, aging studies based solely on cross-sectional comparisons may yield false conclusions. We don't know what 20-year-olds will look like when they are 60, nor do we know what 60-year-olds were like when they were 20. If we want to study the effects of aging we must follow 20-year-olds for the next 40 years, paying special attention to the factors that have been shown to affect health such as exercise, nutrition, stress, and smoking. This would be a longitudinal study and, for obvious reasons, would be very difficult to perform. It wouldn't be correct to draw conclusions about the effects of aging on performance by doing cross-sectional comparisons exclusively. Fortunately, there are scientists who have the stamina to conduct longitudinal studies, and the results of their research are very encouraging with regard to the effects of exercise on the aging process. Let's take a look at some specific changes that take place with aging, and what swimming can do to slow down these changes.

Body Composition

It comes as no surprise that body weight increases with age, but this increase levels off at about age 50. Fortunately, excess body weight is not as detrimental to performance in swimming as it is in other sports such as running and biking. In fact, in a study of 284 female swimmers, percent body fat accounted for less than 4 percent of a swimmer's performance. Even if overall percent body fat remains constant with aging, there is still a redistribution of fat, with peripheral fat decreasing and abdominal fat increasing. In addition, the fat you can feel just under the skin, the subcutaneous fat, decreases, while the internal fat within the muscles and around the organs increases. Although body weight may stabilize past 50 years of age, the percentage of body fat can continue to increase. This is due to a decrease in lean body mass, which consists of muscle, skin, bone, and the organs of the viscera. Between the ages of 40 and 80, women lose lean mass at a rate of 2.5 percent per decade, while men lose even more, at 5 percent per decade. Of course, a decrease in muscle will be detrimental to swimming performance. It has been estimated that physical training can prevent about 25 percent of the loss in lean mass.

Regular physical exercise results in a decrease in fat mass and an increase in muscle mass, regardless of age. This effect

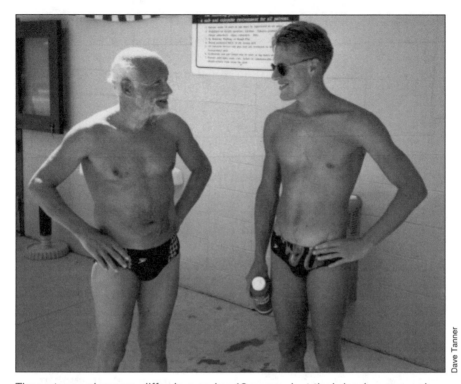

Dave Tanner

These two swimmers differ in age by 40 years, but their body composition is similar.

has even been demonstrated in subjects in their 80s. A case study of two 70-year-old women Masters swimmers showed they had greater muscle strength and lower percent body fat than normal sedentary women in their 70s. In fact, the percent body fat of the swimmers fell within the normal range of women 19 to 25 years old! These results were replicated by the same researchers with a larger sample of 87 women swimmers between the ages of 20 and 69. Again, the percent fat in the highly trained women in both the 50-59 and the 60-69 age groups fell within the normal range for women between 19 and 24 years old. In addition, the older swimmers did not differ from the youngest swimmers in lean body mass.

One of the most noticeable body composition changes with aging is a loss of elasticity in the skin. This is caused by a decrease in peripheral blood flow and a breakdown of collagen and elastin fibers, resulting in thinner, less pliable skin. Chronic exposure to sunlight speeds up this process. Some of the effects of these changes are a decrease in sweat production, less efficient thermoregulation, and increased dryness of the skin. As we shall see later, loss of elasticity in other tissues of the body also affects the lungs, blood vessels, muscles, tendons, and joints.

Cardiovascular Function

While resting heart rate is unaffected by age, maximal heart rate decreases approximately 5 to 10 beats per decade in both men and women, independent of activity level. Training does not change maximal heart rate. The traditional means of estimating maximal heart rate is to subtract your age from 220. For example, a 60-year-old man could expect his maximal heart rate to be around 160 beats/minute. This is a very rough estimate, however, and can range up to 20 beats or more on either side of the predicted number. Not only does maximal heart rate decrease with age but so does the amount of blood the heart can pump with each beat, the stroke volume. Stroke volume is dependent upon the size and contractility of the heart. Because cardiac output, or the amount of blood the heart can pump per minute, is the product of heart rate and stroke volume, the amount of blood the heart can deliver to the muscles during maximal exercise decreases with age. Although swimming does not affect maximal heart rate, it does increase heart size and, therefore, stroke volume and cardiac output. A study of 13 men and 18 women Masters swimmers between the ages of 30 and 78 found cardiac dimensions were not related to age. This means the older swimmers did not have smaller hearts than the younger swimmers. Other documented benefits of regular exercise are decreased resting heart rate, improved peripheral blood flow, lower blood pressure, and increased blood volume that improves stroke volume and cardiac output. Therefore, swimming appears to reduce the age-related declines in all aspects of cardiovascular function.

Of course, muscles depend on the cardiovascular system for their supply of oxygen. One of the consequences of normal aging is an increase in the rigidity of the blood vessels, which results in an increase in blood pressure and a decrease in peripheral blood flow. This decrease in blood flow to the muscles results in decreased oxygen delivery to the muscles.

Less oxygen delivered to the muscles during maximal exercise means the maximal aerobic capacity of the body, or $\dot{V}O_2$max, will be reduced. In fact, numerous cross-sectional studies have shown $\dot{V}O_2$max declines approximately 1 percent per year after the age of 25. However, most of the subjects in these studies were not highly training athletes. Can swimming lower blood pressure and reduce the decline in aerobic capacity? In the study mentioned in the previous paragraph that measured cardiac dimensions, the swimmers did not exhibit the expected increase in blood pressure associated with aging. In the study of 87 female swimmers mentioned in the section on body composition, the decline in $\dot{V}O_2$max was only 7 percent per decade and did not become significant until after the age of 40. In fact, the highly trained women in their 50s and 60s had $\dot{V}O_2$max values comparable to those of sedentary women 20 to 30 years younger.

Pulmonary Function

Loss of elasticity affects pulmonary function as well. Although total lung capacity changes little, the increased rigidity of the lung and chest wall tissues results in a decrease in the amount of air that can be expired quickly, the forced expiratory volume, and an increase in the amount of air left in the lungs after a complete exhalation, the residual volume. The larger residual volume results in a decrease in vital capacity, the volume of air that can be exhaled following a complete inhalation. The result of these changes is a decrease in the maximal ventilatory capacity of the pulmonary system, both in terms of respiratory frequency and total volume per minute. These decreases contribute to the decline in $\dot{V}O_2$max and may limit intense aerobic activity. Swimming has been shown to maintain vital capacity and increase the strength and endurance of the respiratory muscles. The resulting increase in ventilatory capacity contributes toward reducing the usual 1 percent per year decline in $\dot{V}O_2$max seen in sedentary subjects.

Muscles and Nerves

The peak years for muscular strength are from 25 to 35. As muscle mass decreases with age, the number of muscle fibers decreases as a result of atrophy. Fast-twitch fibers seem to be affected more than slow-twitch fibers. Fast-twitch fibers are the fibers we use to do quick, explosive movements, movements a normal sedentary 50-year-old doesn't do very often. It's no wonder the fast-twitch fibers atrophy; they're no longer needed. We therefore see a greater decline in rapid velocity contractions than in slow velocity contractions, and a greater decline in strength than endurance. Women experience greater declines in strength than men do.

Not only is there less muscle, but the metabolic characteristics of the muscle change with age. There is a decrease in the enzymes that are involved in oxidation, the process that uses oxygen to produce the energy needed for muscular contraction. The result is a decrease in the aerobic capacity of the muscle, another contributor to the age-related decline in $\dot{V}O_2$max and swimming endurance.

The decrease in muscle mass also results in a decrease in anaerobic capacity, the ability to provide energy to the muscles without the use of oxygen via a process known as glycolysis. A metabolic intermediary in this process is lactic acid. As people age, lactic acid production declines because the muscle fibers that rely more on glycolysis are the fast-twitch fibers, those that are preferentially lost with aging. These are also the muscle fibers that are most important in sprint events such as the 50. Not only is less lactic acid produced, but the decline in peripheral blood flow reduces its removal from the muscle. The point at which lactate begins to accumulate in the blood as exercise intensity increases is called the lactate threshold. It is a balance between lactate production and lactate removal. In untrained individuals it typically occurs at a level of intensity corresponding to 50-60% of maximal aerobic capacity, but it occurs at a lower intensity in older adults than in young adults. Because swimming events lasting less than two minutes depend heavily on the anaerobic system for energy, its decline with age seriously affects performance.

The anaerobic system can be maintained through lifelong training. In a study conducted before the 1988 World Masters Swimming Championships, swimmers aged 46 to 56+ did not differ from 25- to 35-year-old swimmers in their ability to produce and remove lactic acid. It has been suggested that maintenance of muscle mass, especially the glycolytic fast-twitch fibers, is responsible for the maintenance of the anaerobic system. However, in order to achieve these results, high-intensity training must be performed, something the typical person 50 or over doesn't do very often.

We've seen that regular exercise, like swimming, is very effective at reducing the age-related declines in aerobic and anaerobic capacity. The news is even better when we consider muscular function. Numerous studies have demonstrated that adults of all ages who participate in carefully structured weight-lifting programs are stronger than their sedentary cohorts. Even women in their 80s respond to weight training. Because swimming is a sport in which strength is especially important, we'll dedicate an entire chapter to the benefits of strength training toward improved performance.

Flexibility in a joint declines rapidly if the muscles that cross that joint aren't stretched through participation in physical activity. The muscle shortens and the range of motion of the joint is reduced. The fact that flexibility declines at a very early age (middle 20s) suggests this decline may be attributed more to a lack of activity than to aging. There is, however, a decrease in flexibility with age due to increased rigidity of the muscle connective tissue and tendons. Exercise improves flexibility, however. Women swimmers in their 70s have been shown to have greater flexibility than less active women of the same age, and were within the range one would expect for much younger women.

Nerves also are affected by age. Neural control decreases and the muscle becomes less excitable, meaning it does not respond to an electrical stimulus as quickly as when it was younger. Its peak isometric force is lower and it takes longer to reach peak force. Some nerves disintegrate completely, with the greatest functional loss in the largest and fastest fibers. Again, daily use of these nerves through swimming helps to counteract the atrophy associated with aging.

In short, almost all of the body's physiological systems decline in function with age. If we relate these declines to performance, we see a decline in endurance and a decline in strength, although endurance is less affected than strength. Most of the decline with age is due to a sedentary lifestyle and cannot be attributed to aging itself. The rate of aging is very much dependent upon the level of one's physical inactivity.

These past-50 swimmers are more physically fit than the average person 40 years younger!

Exercise Slows the Aging Process

By now the message that regular exercise slows the aging process should be loud and clear. Can a lifetime of training maintain the endurance and strength of youth? Research suggests the rewards are worth the effort. We have seen that many of the physiological characteristics that we use to measure fitness, such as body composition, aerobic capacity, and strength, are similar between a sedentary 25-year-old and a well-trained 70-year-old. Chronological age is often a poor predictor of physiological function for an individual, especially in a technical sport such as swimming. This is great news for all of you who use swimming to hold off aging.

Most of the research that has investigated the effects of exercise on aging has been cross-sectional, a comparison of today's 70-year-olds with today's 25-year-olds, for example. Ideally, we'd like to be able to follow a group of 25-year-old swimmers through their lives to see how they change by the time they are 70. In this way we could get a much better picture of how swimming affects aging. The results certainly would be encouraging because age-related declines are substantially less when performances are measured longitudinally instead of cross-sectionally. Unfortunately, very little longitudinal research has been conducted with swimmers. However, it has been done with runners. Dr. David Costill of the Human Performance Laboratory at Ball State University conducted a 22-year longitudinal study of the age-related decline in $\dot{V}O_2$max in 53 runners between the ages of 40 and 75. The average decline was 6 percent per decade, a value very similar to the 7 percent decline in women swimmers mentioned earlier. Those who trained the most during the previous 22 years experienced the smallest decline in $\dot{V}O_2$max. Furthermore, the two men who trained most consistently showed almost no decline at all. More importantly, the men who had trained consistently saw no increase in the oxygen cost of submaximal running despite a decrease in their maximal aerobic capacity, suggesting that only the upper limit of their exercise range had declined in 22 years.

Ten of these runners were classified as "fit old," meaning their average age was 68 at the end of the study and they had maintained a high level of fitness for the past 20 to 25 years. Although their body weight did not change over that period of time, lean body mass decreased and fat mass increased. The decline in aerobic capacity for this group was 15 percent per decade, despite continued training. Before becoming too discouraged by this result, keep in mind these were elite runners at the time of the first testing. Therefore, they had more aerobic capacity to lose than the normal moderately active men of their age. Also, it was reported they had reduced their training distance and intensity during the 22 years of the study. All told, the 15 percent decline in $\dot{V}O_2$max cannot be attributed entirely to aging. Other longitudinal studies conducted on non-elite runners have shown no difference in $\dot{V}O_2$max in men as old as 62 after 10 years of consistent training.

Why do we care so much about maximal aerobic capacity anyway? How often do we exercise maximally? The really encouraging point to take from the Costill study is that submaximal oxygen consumption at a given workload did not change in 22 years! The other bright point to remember from all of this research is that the well-trained past-50 swimmer, despite the physiological changes that take place with aging, is as fit or fitter than sedentary people 30 or more years younger. When we consider that some of the measures of fitness can decline by up to 50 percent in only three weeks of detraining, we should be encouraged by the much smaller declines seen in adults who train consistently over decades. You may not be the same person physically that you were at the age of 25, but you are certainly better than you would be if you didn't swim.

The Potential of the Past-50 Swimmer

We've only begun to realize the potential of the past-50 swimmer. In 1979, at age 58, while training to become the oldest person to swim the English Channel, Doc Counsilman summarized the potential of the older athlete.

> As you get older you tend to get out of shape due to our social structure. You have to work. You neglect your body. You don't have 2, 3, 4 hours a day to devote to exercise. Older athletes have a tremendous amount of potential. I'm talking about people my age. I'm 58. We have so much potential in our body and we've lost it due to lack of exercise. It's taken me a year and a half to train for the Channel and I'm swimming times now that I never swam when I was in college. But I personally feel that in the next 100 years we will see men 50 years old running under 4 minutes in the mile and I think we'll see 50-year-old men swimming under 4 minutes for 400 meters. That's how convinced I am that there's just untapped physical potential in older people.

Indeed, it may not take 100 years to reach these goals. A 41-year-old ma has already broken four minutes in the mile. Doc's prediction in swimming may be more difficult to fulfill, as the fastest 400-meter freestyle by a 50-year-old to date has been only 4:43.72.

Since its inception in 1970, Masters swimming has led the way in demonstrating the potential of the older athlete. Record times in the upper age groups have steadily declined as swimmers over 50 train harder and wiser. As an example, consider the progression of the national record times for the 50-54 age group from 1972 to 1997. In figure 2.1 we see that the women's 100-yard freestyle record dropped from 1:10.80 to 59.05, while the men's record fell from 57.52 to 50.14. The situation is even more striking in the 1,650-yard freestyle (figure 2.2). The women's record dropped from 27:46.72 to 20:08.75, while the men's record went down to 18:21.85 from 21:51.2 in 1972. These are tremendous improvements in only 25 years. In a few instances the same person broke his or her own record year after year. As these athletes aged, they swam

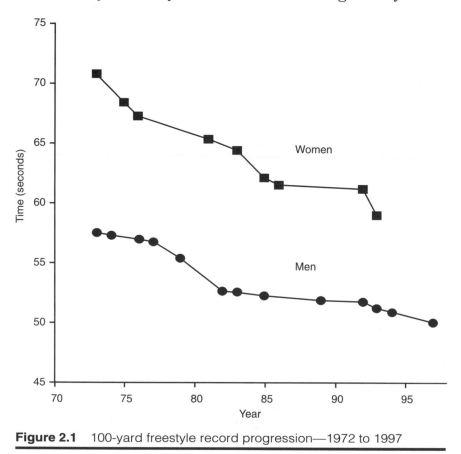

Figure 2.1   100-yard freestyle record progression—1972 to 1997

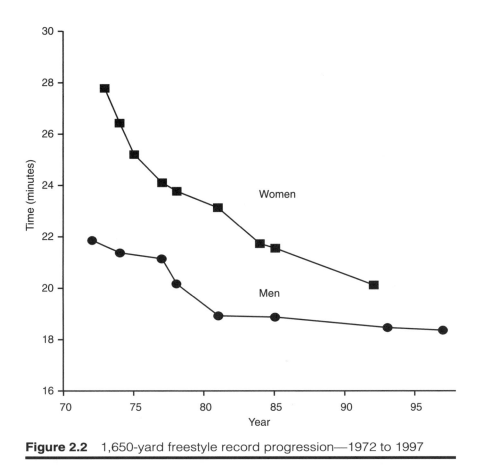

Figure 2.2 1,650-yard freestyle record progression—1972 to 1997

faster! These swimmers are tapping into their physical potential. The same phenomenon has occurred in the higher age groups as well. In fact, the current 60-64 age group records in the 100 and 1,650 are faster now than the 50-54 age group records were in 1972! Clearly the past-50 swimmer is performing better and better.

Is there a limit to how fast the past-50 swimmer can go? The graphs suggest the rate of improvement is slowing down. Realistically, past the age of 50 there is a limit to how much physical capacity can be increased by training. We will not see huge changes as a result of working out longer. Further improvements in the records will occur, but they will be due to more carefully structured training both in the pool and in the weight room, more attention to correct stroke mechanics, more opportunities to compete, and an increase in the expectations of what a past-50 swimmer can accomplish. The record holders have set the standards for everyone else. Even if the records improve more slowly than the onslaught that has occurred over the past 30 years, the pack at the top will get tighter as more people reach their athletic potential.

ARDETH MUELLER

Home: St Louis, MO
Current age group: 55 to 59
Started Masters swimming at age 35.

As a youngster Ardeth participated in a summer-only swim program from age 8 to age 16. The 1976 Masters nationals held in St. Louis brought her back to the sport. She's been destroying the competition ever since, recording her best performances from ages 43 through 49. In 1997 Ardeth was elected to the Swimming Hall of Fame as a Masters swimmer.

Ardeth swims five times a week at about 4,500 yards per workout. Her dryland training consists of 30 minutes on a rowing machine and 30 minutes on the stair master four times a week. She trains with a coach at the Rockwood Masters and appreciates the value of being part of a large group from St. Louis supporting each other at the meets.

I swim because I like the way it makes me feel. I enjoy the people I have met and the people I have become friends with over the years. I believe there is a spiritual side to swimming that is as important as the physical fitness benefits. It is the one time during the day that I am able to live in the moment and find peace regardless of what else is happening in my life. I thank God every day for this special gift. I hope to continue swimming and training until I'm in the 90+ age group.

Ardeth's Sample Workout
(Written by her coach, Thomas Huggins):

3 × 300 Fly (no free) on 5:00

3 × 100 IM on 1:45

4 × 50 Kick Fly on 1:00

30 sec rest

3 × 200 Fly on 4:00

3 × 100 IM on 1:45

4 × 50 Kick Fly on 1:00

30 sec rest

3 × 100 Fly on 1:50

3 × 100 IM on 1:45

4 × 50 Kick Fly on 1:00

No wonder she holds the World Record!

chapter

3

The Basics of
Swim Training

Serious training for any sport can be a very complicated subject, and swimming is no exception. Although the basic concepts of training are fairly simple, they sound complicated because of the mountain of nomenclature that has been heaped upon them. In its simplest form, swim training consists of the typical workout of the fitness swimmer, continuous swimming at a constant, moderate pace. At the other end of the spectrum are the seven training levels, based on energy systems, designed by United States Swimming, the governing organization of elite swimming in the United States. We'll take the middle ground and present a brief overview of swim training in a way that's easy to understand, with an emphasis on the special concerns of the older athlete.

As coaches, we've been impressed by the interest expressed by our past-50 swimmers in the latest principles and methods of training. They soak up everything we can give them. As we shall see, the brute force method of training used by younger swimmers—more training volume—will not produce the same results in the past-50 swimmer. Smarter training is the key to success, and the swimmers we've coached are very cognizant of this fact. They want to know everything they can about the best way to train, given the limited amount of time and energy they can devote to the sport. For one reason or another, many past-50 swimmers never have had the opportunity to use the newer training methods described below. Perhaps they are new to organized swim training, or perhaps these methods were not available to them in their youth. We see tremendous improvements in performance in our past-50 swimmers who are finally able to train in a modern way. You *can* teach an old dog new tricks!

When we coach a group of swimmers of different ages, we modify the workout based on skill level, not age. It's not uncommon for the best past-50 swimmers to outperform many of the under-30 youngsters in the pool. Remember from the previous chapter that a well trained 50-year-old may be physiologically very similar to a much younger athlete. Nevertheless, we do make some concessions to the past-50 swimmer because of the differences in how these two athletes respond to training. We concede that compared with a younger swimmer, the older swimmer will not improve as much with training. In addition, the older swimmer requires more training to reach the same level of fitness as the younger swimmer. By more training we mean it takes more weeks of training and more distance in the pool to get the same results. The past-50 swimmer also takes longer to recover because the older body is slower to adapt. Therefore, we schedule more rest in the training programs of our past-50 swimmers. Unfortunately, the older athlete also loses conditioning more quickly. In fact, the older you are, the faster you lose it. The bottom line is that the older swimmer must train more *consistently* and allow more *recovery* time, as paradoxical as that sounds. To gain the maximum benefit, the structure of a training program for the past-50 swimmer must be planned very carefully.

Stress and Adaptation

The entire basis of training for any sport revolves around the principle of stress and adaptation described by Hans Selye in his 1956 book *The Stress of Life*. He called it the General Adaptation Syndrome (GAS). Dr. Selye used mice to study the effects of stress, but his principle applies to humans as well. When a stress is placed on an organism, it attempts to adapt to that stress. The type of adaptation depends on the form of the stress. Stresses take many forms: physical, mental, emotional, dietary, etc. In athletics, stress takes the form of a training stimulus. Adaptation occurs if the body is capable of resisting this stress. The organism becomes stronger. Furthermore, it adapts to specific stresses in specific ways. Herein lies the science of designing a training program. This is the reason we have so many different types of training. Each training stress, or stimulus, is designed to elicit a specific response. The key to a successful program is to apply the stimulus that will result in the desired adaptation. For example, if you want to be a better sprinter, the training stimulus should be of the sprint type. An over-distance stimulus will not result in better sprint performance.

Dr. Selye demonstrated that if he placed too much stress on his mice they became ill or died. They failed to adapt. Likewise, if the human body cannot adapt to the stress of training, exhaustion occurs, resulting in poor performance, injury, or illness. The goal in training, therefore, is to apply sufficient stimulus to elicit the desired training response without creating so much stress that the body fails to adapt. Signs of failed adaptation can be physical and mental. Some of the mild symptoms include poor performance, elevated resting heart rate, irritability, and loss of appetite. More severe symptoms include aching muscles, exhaustion, inability to sleep, and weight loss. The earliest indicators of impending failure are mood disturbances and a lack of interest in training. Because it takes so long to recover, the past-50 swimmer should be especially watchful of these symptoms to avoid the stage of failed adaptation. So, if you wake up in a bad mood and don't feel like swimming, don't swim!

How to Use a Pace Clock

All the training methods we use are based on distance and time. Distance is easy to determine in a pool. Time, however, requires a clock of some sort. Years ago, times were called out by a coach on the deck holding a stopwatch. The most significant technical advancement toward facilitating the variety of training methods we use today was the invention of the pace clock, the big white clocks with the three-foot faces found in most pools. By giving swimmers the ability to time themselves easily, the pace clock finally allowed the coach the freedom to do some actual coaching. Pace clocks are especially useful to the older swimmer who is more likely to be swimming alone without a coach. These clocks are also an excellent gauge of training intensity, a task performed by the heart rate monitor in other sports such as running and cycling. Although most heart rate monitors are designed to be waterproof, their use in swimming isn't widespread. The pace clock is just so much more convenient, and cheaper, too.

The standard pace clock has two hands, one for minutes and one for seconds. In our pool, the minute hand is set for the time of day so our swimmers can tell what time it is without having to wear a watch. The minute hand is useful to fitness swimmers for timing long distance swims. The second hand is used for timing short interval swims. Using a pace clock to time

A pace clock can be found in most lap swimming pools.

yourself is simple. For ease in figuring out your time at the end of a swim it is best to start swimming when the second hand is in the 12 o'clock position ("on the 60" or "on the top") or in the 6 o'clock position ("on the 30" or "on the bottom"). "On the 15" and "on the 45" correspond to the 3 o'clock and 9 o'clock positions, respectively. On short swims you'll be able to determine your total time without considering the position of the minute hand, but on longer swims you may need to check your pace midway through the distance. That's why it's called a "pace" clock.

Interval training is especially dependent upon the use of a pace clock. Swimmers have developed a shorthand lingo to make communication easier. Suppose the workout set consists of four repetitions of 50 yards with a 10-second rest interval between each repeat, starting on the 60. This is written as "4 × 50 with 10 seconds rest." You would start when the second hand is on the 60 (top), swim 50 yards, then look at the clock to get your time. Suppose it was 55 seconds. By the time your 10 seconds of rest are up, the second hand will be on the 5, or 1 o'clock position of the clock. Time to go again! You continue in this manner, resting exactly 10 seconds after each 50 until you've completed four repeats. Notice that no matter how fast or how slow you go, you always get 10 seconds rest between 50s.

This set could also be done on a "fixed interval," meaning you would start each 50 at a fixed interval of time following the *beginning* of the previous 50. Let's say the fixed interval is 1:05 so you'll be swimming a 50 every 65 seconds. Now the set is written like this: "4 × 50 on 1:05." Again you start on the 60 and swim the first 50. But now, no matter how slow or fast you go, the next 50 starts when the second hand is on the 5. Note the distinction between leaving "on 1:05" and leaving "on the 5." The former is the fixed interval while the latter is the position of the second hand. To avoid this confusion some swimmers say "at 1:05," meaning at a fixed interval of 1:05 between repeats, instead of "on 1:05." After completing the second 50 you wait until the second hand is on the 10 before starting the third 50. The fourth 50 will start on the 15. The fixed interval method of using a pace clock is much more structured than the rest interval method and is preferred by most coaches. Clever swimmers can determine even how many repeats they have done by knowing the position of the second hand when they start the next repeat. You now know the basics of using a pace clock, enough to understand the sample workouts in chapter 9.

It Takes Energy to Exercise

In order to understand the purpose behind each type of training we must know something about the energy sources for exercise. The only source of energy for muscular contraction is a molecule called adenosine triphosphate, or ATP. At any one instant we have only about five seconds worth of ATP, so it must be constantly replaced as it is used. The three systems that regenerate ATP—oxidation, glycolysis, and phosphocreatine (ATP-PCr)—are described on the next page. Swimming is a sport that relies heavily on all three systems to supply energy to the working muscles, muscles that must satisfy three performance requirements: endurance, sustained speed, and explosive speed. These three qualities correspond roughly to the oxidative, glycolytic, and ATP-PCr systems. Endurance, which is the ability to exercise for a long period of time, is fueled primarily by the oxidative system. Slow-twitch fibers tend to be more oxidative and therefore have more endurance. Sustained speed, which is the ability to exercise maximally for periods lasting from about 20 seconds up to two minutes, is fueled primarily by the glycolytic system, with help from the oxidative system toward the end of the two-minute period. Finally, explosive speed, which is the ability to sprint fast for short periods less than 20 seconds, is fueled by the ATP-PCr system, with help from the glycolytic system toward the end of the 20-second period. Slow-twitch and fast-twitch muscle fibers have distinct metabolic characteristics. Slow fibers tend to be more oxidative in nature and therefore have more endurance than fast fibers, but are not as strong. Fast fibers tend to be better at glycolysis and have more PCr, so they are faster and stronger but fatigue more quickly. Clearly the fast fibers are very important for swimming performance. Unfortunately, they atrophy at a higher rate than the slow fibers as you age. You will have to focus your attention on these fibers in your training program in order to keep them.

THE THREE ENERGY SYSTEMS

Oxidation: the aerobic system. Oxidation takes place in the mitochondria of the muscle cell, where it is used to regenerate ATP, with carbon dioxide and water given off as by-products. Oxidation yields 36 ATP per molecule of glucose. Oxidation can continue indefinitely, as long as the mitochondria are supplied with fuel and the by-products are removed. Clearly, oxidation is our best choice for regenerating ATP. In swimming it's the primary energy source for events lasting longer than two minutes and plays a significant role in shorter events as well. Energy for recovery from any event comes entirely from oxidation. Aerobic capacity improves substantially with training, at any age.

Glycolysis: also known as the lactic acid or anaerobic lactate system. Although glycolysis is twice as fast as oxidation, it produces 18 times less energy. Two ATP molecules are generated in the process of breaking down a molecule of glucose into two molecules of pyruvate. The pyruvate then enters the mitochondria to fuel oxidation. If the demand for energy is great, i.e., the intensity of exercise is very high, glycolysis will generate more pyruvate than the mitochondria can handle, so a bottleneck occurs. In order to allow glycolysis to continue producing ATP, the extra pyruvate is converted to lactic acid, which diffuses into the blood as lactate. Glycolysis is most effective from about 20 seconds to two minutes of all-out exercise, corresponding to the 50 and 100 events in swimming. Past two minutes, glycolysis no longer can meet the high energy demands of the muscle, so intensity must be reduced to match the energy available via oxidation. The glycolytic system improves substantially with training, at any age.

ATP-PCr system: also known as the immediate or anaerobic alactate system. Energy derived from phosphocreatine (PCr) is used to produce ATP. This system is twice as fast as glycolysis, but only one ATP molecule is generated for each molecule of PCr. Although very fast, the PCr is exhausted in a very short time, approximately 10 seconds, by which time glycolysis has taken over the energy needs of the muscle. In swimming this system is used during the dive and the first few meters of a race. The ATP-PCr system is highly dependent upon the genetically determined characteristics of the muscle fiber and responds only slightly to training.

Pool events in swimming range from 50 meters to 1,500 meters, lasting in duration from approximately 30 seconds to almost 30 minutes, while open water swims and triathlons range in distance from about 800 meters to 20 miles or more. However, the events most people swim (50 and 100 yards/ meters) are in the 30-second to two-minute range, the energy domain shared by glycolysis and oxidation. Our training therefore should emphasize these two systems. We can't ignore the ATP-PCr system, however. One glance at the elite athletes in our sport tells us strength is important. They *look* strong. They also move very quickly. We would say they're powerful. Power is defined as the product of strength (the ability to generate force) and speed of movement. Swimming is a power sport. If we run a statistical correlation between the various physiological qualities involved in performance—strength, speed, power, aerobic capacity, anaerobic capacity, body composition—the quality with the highest correlation with performance is power. The swimmers that can generate the most power are the ones that perform the best. The muscle fibers that generate the most power are the fast-twitch fibers, the fibers high in PCr, and unfortunately, the same fibers that are preferentially lost with aging. Clearly, you must keep power in mind when you design your training program.

The Five Types of Training

The five types of training we present here were defined and refined by Doc Counsilman during his long coaching career from 1946 to 1991. Before Doc, swim training had very little structure. A typical workout consisted of straight swimming, followed by a few sprints. Today the variety of combinations of these training methods is almost unlimited, to the point where designing a workout correctly is a real challenge. Table 3.1 gives a summary of the five basic types of training used in swimming today: over-distance, speed play, interval, goal sets, and sprint. A more complete description can be found in *The New Science of Swimming* by James E. and Brian E. Counsilman, or many of the other books listed in the bibliography. The nomenclature may vary from reference to reference, but the basic concepts are the same. The purpose is to apply a specific training stimulus and, no matter what you call it, the resulting physical adaptation is the same.

Over-Distance Training

Over-distance training is the oldest type of swim training. As its name implies, an over-distance swim is longer than race distance, at a constant speed that is slower than race pace.

Table 3.1

THE FIVE TYPES OF SWIM TRAINING (AS DEFINED BY COUNSILMAN)

Type of Training	Energy System	Quality Developed
Over-distance	Oxidation	Endurance
Speed Play	Oxidation, some glycolysis	Endurance, some sustained speed
Interval	Oxidation, glycolysis	Endurance, sustained speed
Goal Sets	Glycolysis, ATP-PCr, some oxidation	Sustained speed, strength, some endurance
Sprint	ATP-PCr, glycolysis	Explosive speed, strength

Since the energy source for this type of exercise is oxidation, over-distance training improves the aerobic system, and hence endurance. Besides endurance, over-distance training helps you learn how to swim at a steady pace and improves your confidence in your ability to swim long distances. A lap swimmer who comes to the pool and swims for a mile at a steady pace is doing over-distance training exclusively. Other examples include kicking 500 yards easy or pulling 1,000 yards at a moderate but steady pace. A 1,500-meter time trial also would be classified as over-distance training.

This type of training does very little to improve speed. The positive aspect of over-distance training is that it can be done successfully by a swimmer of any age or skill level. Although it is an important aspect of everyone's training program, over-distance training has contributed to swimming's reputation as a "boring" sport. Unless you really enjoy the water, swimming back and forth at a constant pace can become rather monotonous. The only scenery is a black line on the bottom of the pool, and there is no social interaction with others. If you're currently a lap swimmer, you'll be doing yourself a favor by interspersing the other types of training into your program.

Speed Play Training

Speed play training, also known as Fartlek training after the Swedish word for speed play, is a modification of over-distance training involving alternate fast and slow efforts. By increasing speed for short periods during a continuous swim you stimulate the glycolytic system as well as oxidation. Although speed play training primarily improves endurance, the short bursts of faster pace will somewhat benefit sustained speed as well. This type of training became popular in swimming in the 1930s and is still used extensively today. Swimming 800, every third

JACK GEOGHEGAN

Home: Rye, New York
Current age group: 55 to 59
Started Masters swimming at age 31.

Jack started swimming in a summer club at age 10, but by his own admission "was never very good." He also played football, baseball, and basketball in grade school, but was too small for football in high school so he ran cross country and played basketball and baseball. He continued to swim twice a week for one hour and had a best time of 1:02 in the 100 freestyle by his senior year in high school. That summer he swam with the Badger Sports Club under Jack Collins, doing workouts given to them by Doc Counsilman. By the time he got to Villanova University he had a good background and in four years dropped his times to 22.0 in the 50, 47.4 in the 100, and 1:46.8 in the 200. He then retired to coaching the Rye YMCA Boys swim team. During this time he continued to participate in touch football, volleyball, squash, skiing, racquetball, tennis, and paddle tennis. Recently he has taken up the sport of golf.

© Carl House

Jack came back to swimming competition at the 1973 Masters nationals in Chicago. He gave his best performances as he turned 40, when he put full concentration on the sport, often working out twice a day. He received a good deal of notoriety for breaking 50 seconds in the 100 freestyle, which in 1982 was an incredible feat for a 40-year-old man. He recorded many lifetime best performances that year, including a 4-second drop in the 100 breast-stroke.

I have continued to strive to keep as close as possible to the 50 second mark for the 100 freestyle as I believe that is retarding the aging process and will allow me to party for an extended period.

Jack trains five days per week (Mon, Tues, Thurs, Fri, & Sat), sharing coaching duties with Dave Samuelson and Mike Laux. Thursday is fin day, a day dedicated almost entirely to kicking, usually with longer fins, sometimes Zoomers. Workouts average 3,000–3,500 yards. He always does the same warm-up: 1,000 yards as 200 free swim, 400 IM kick, 200 back swim, and 200 free pull, both before workouts and meets. At meets he adds sprints. He enjoys pull sets, mostly using a buoy, a tube around his ankles, and hand paddles. Sample sets: 4 × 400 on 5 min, 10 × 100 on 1:15, 10 × 50 on :35. He does a lot of IM work and stroke drills concentrating on long freestyle for low stroke count per lap, hip rotation on backstroke, long glide phase in breast, few kicks per lap, and hip-up fly also with few strokes per lap. Before major competitions he always uses a "gauge" set to determine how his conditioning has gone: 5 × 100 free pull on 1:30 with full gear, looking for 1:05 pace. He doesn't lift regularly, but tries to get a circuit routine at the local Y twice a week from January through March. "I usually fail to keep the schedule," he says.

Swimming allows me to eat, drink, and be merry without concerns of weight gain. It alleviates the stresses of everyday life and business. While I dislike the early 6 am workouts, it does really get the day off to a good start. Not to be trite, but it is a clean sport and relatively inexpensive. The participants are bright, interesting people with a zest for life and a proper balance in their lives. I've never met a swimmer I didn't like.

Jack's Sample Workout:

Warm-up: 200 free swim, 400 IM kick, 200 back swim, 200 free pull

10 × 50 drill on 60 - Kick down, swim back

IM Drills: one arm fly, rifle arm backstroke, long glide/few kicks breaststroke, half catch-up freestyle

500 free pull hypoxic 3-5-7-5-3 breathing pattern by 100s

5 × 200 swim, alternate IM, free, reverse IM, back, IM

6 × 25 down no breath, back easy

Cool-down: A few lengths of easy swimming

length fast, is an example of speed play. Swimming one length hard followed by one length easy, two hard, two easy, three hard, three easy, four hard, four easy, and back down again is another way to "play" with an 800. This method is called a locomotor. Speed play training is appropriate for swimmers of any age and skill level.

Interval Training

The big leap in improved training methods occurred in 1939, but it wasn't in the sport of swimming. It was in running. In that year, German track coach Woldemar Gerschler applied his "Controlled Interval Method" of training to propel Rudolph Harbig to world record times of 46.0 and 1:46.6 in the 400-meter and 800-meter runs, respectively. These were outrageously fast performances for that era, and the rest of the world took note. Gerschler's method involved runs of submaximal effort followed by short intervals of rest whose duration was controlled by heart rate, hence the name "Controlled Interval Method." The key was to start the next effort before complete recovery was achieved. After World War II, interval training flooded the running world and eventually seeped into the swimming pools. Promoted by Doc Counsilman and others, interval training quickly became the mainstay of most high-level swimming programs in the world. To this day, with innumerable variations, it continues to be the most widely used type of swim training.

Interval training is the antidote to the boredom of over-distance training. The energy systems used and the qualities developed depend on the four factors that define interval training. They are the distance of each repeat, the interval of rest between repeats, the number of repetitions in each set, and the speed, or time, for each repeat. These factors can be easily remembered by the acronym DIRT: Distance, Interval, Rest, and Time. Combinations of DIRT are almost limitless. The type of training stimulus desired will determine the values of the DIRT variables. If the goal is to develop endurance, then the rest interval should be short and the effort moderate. These are called "slow" intervals, and they consist of a low rest-to-work ratio. An example might be a set of 10 × 50 with 15 seconds rest. A swimmer who takes one minute to complete each 50 has a rest-to-work ratio of 15 to 60, or 1 to 4. To develop more sustained speed, the rest should be increased so the time to perform each repeat can be decreased. For example, the swimmer may do the same set of 50s in a faster time, say 50 seconds each, if one minute of rest is allowed between repeats. This would be a rest-to-work ratio of 60 to 50, or approximately 1 to 1. The dividing line is a little fuzzy, but rest-to-work ratios of 1:1 or higher are termed "fast" intervals and are more appropriate for developing sustained speed. More examples of the different types of interval sets are presented on the next page.

The key to effective interval training is to allow only incomplete recovery during the rest interval. This means the rest must not be too long. The advantage of interval training over swimming continuously is that higher intensity work can be performed. The energy stores of the muscles can be partially, but not completely, replenished during the short rest period in preparation for the next effort. Interval training is appropriate for all swimmers because the DIRT variables can be easily modified to accommodate for age and skill level. Compared to straight swimming, interval training is also a good motivational tool. It's much easier to complete a long swim if you break the workout into smaller segments with rest in between. If you train by yourself, you can challenge the pace clock to a competition, instead of the person in the next lane.

Goal Set Training

Goal set training also has been called lactate training and repetition training. It differs from interval training in that it features a longer rest interval between efforts, allowing near-complete recovery. Here, the effort is near-maximal. Because the distance swum is usually the same as that swum in a race, i.e., 50, 100, or 200, the energy systems used are the same as those used in a race, mostly glycolysis with some ATP-PCr and oxidation. This is the most specific type of training in relation to a real race. It is therefore the best way to learn how to pace a race, aside from actually doing the race in a meet. Goal set training can be thought of as repeated time trials, hence the name repetition training is often applied. The name "goal set" indicates that a time goal for each repeat is usually specified.

TYPES OF INTERVAL TRAINING DEMONSTRATING WAYS THAT DISTANCE, INTERVAL, REST, AND TIME (DIRT) CAN BE VARIED

Straight Set of Repeats: Constant distance, interval, and time, set gets harder at end because of fatigue
Example:　10 × 100 on 2:00, hold steady average

Decreasing Distance Repeats: Decrease distance, increase effort/speed
Example:　400 look at 300 time on the way but don't stop, rest 1:00
　　　　　300 faster than first 300 of 400 above, look at 200 time, rest 1:00
　　　　　200 faster than first 200 of 300 above, look at 100 time, rest 1:00
　　　　　100 faster than first 100 of 200 above
Example:　Ladder: 200, 150, 100, 50, 50, 100 150, 200, rest 30 seconds

Mixed Set: Vary distance and interval (interval remains consistent when expressed per 100, i.e., 2:00)
Example:　1 × 400 on 8:00
　　　　　2 × 200 on 4:00
　　　　　4 × 100 on 2:00
　　　　　8 × 50 on 1:00

Descending Rest: Constant distance, decrease interval of rest, increase effort by necessity
Example:　5 × 100 on 2:00
　　　　　5 × 100 on 1:50
　　　　　5 × 100 on 1:40
Example:　Descending time 50s (1st on 1:00, 2nd on :59, 3rd on :58 etc. until failure)

Increasing Rest: Constant distance, increased interval of rest, increased effort (more rest)
Example:　5 × 100, 1st on 1:45, 2nd on 1:50, 3rd on 1:55, 4th on 2:00

Descending Time Set: Constant distance and interval, increase effort
Example:　5 × 100 on 2:00, descend speed from 1:45 on 1st to 1:30 on last

Ascending Time Set: Constant distance and interval, decrease effort (good for cooldown)
Example:　5 × 100 on 2:00, ascend from 1:30 to 1:45

Alternating Descend/Ascend: Constant distance and interval, vary effort
Example:　10 × 100 on 2:00, descend the even ones, ascend the odd ones

Alternating Slow/Fast Set: Constant distance and interval, alternate effort— hard/easy, active recovery
Example:　10 × 50 Every Other One Fast (EOOF), fast ones on 3:00

Broken Set: Break distance into equal segments but think of it as a straight swim with short rest
Example:　400 Broken into 4 × 100 with 15 seconds rest, subtract rest time (:45) from total to get 400 time
Example:　200 Broken into 4 × 50 with 10 seconds rest, subtract rest time (:30) from total to get 200 time

Simulators: Like broken set but decrease distance of segments to simulate a race
Example:　200 Broken, race pace (100 rest 20 seconds, 50 rest 10 seconds, 2 × 25 rest 5 seconds)
Example:　1,500 Broken into 500, 400, 300, 200, 100 rest 10 seconds

Because the effort is near-maximal, above the lactate threshold, the alternate name of "lactate" training often is used. Goal set training often is confused with interval training. The key difference is the amount of recovery allowed. Interval training permits only incomplete recovery between repeats, whereas goal set training allows near-complete recovery. For example, a set of 5 × 100 with 30 seconds rest between each 100 is interval training, but the same set (done from a dive) with five minutes rest between repeats is goal set training. The training stimuli of the two sets are different, and so are the resulting adaptations. Other examples are 10 × 50 (from a dive) on 3:00, and 3 × 200 on 10:00. Because this type of training is very stressful and can result in fatigue that lasts for days, the past-50 swimmer should use it sparingly. A goal set once every two weeks during the high-intensity phase of the season is a reasonable guideline. The number and intensity of repeats can be modified to accommodate skill level. Goal set training is just

Sprinting uses the fast-twitch muscle fibers.

like swimming in a meet and is very fatiguing. Allow plenty of time for recovery before doing it again, just as you would after a meet.

Sprint Training

Sprint training differs from goal set training in that sprints are shorter than race distance, 100 percent efforts, at faster than race pace. Sprints are usually 25 meters or less. Sprinting relies on the ATP-PCr and glycolytic energy systems and develops explosive speed and strength. Examples include swimming 25 repeats all out with long rest or 12-yard sprints from a dive. Sprints are very important for the past-50 swimmer because they help to maintain the fast-twitch muscle fibers that are so easily lost during aging. They should be done in moderation throughout the season.

In the next chapter we will explain how to combine these five types of training into an integrated workout plan.

chapter 4

Designing a Training Program

In the early years of competitive swimming, before the introduction of interval, speed play, and goal set training, designing a training program was fairly straightforward. Scientists only were beginning to understand the complex physiological adaptations that occur with different forms of training. For example, a typical workout in the era of Johnny Weissmuller consisted primarily of over-distance work: continuous swimming, kicking, pulling, some turns, and maybe a couple of sprints. The majority of his practice time was devoted to perfecting technique. His many world record performances are even more amazing, considering he did them with training that, today, we'd consider no more than a warm-up. Imagine what he might have accomplished with modern training principles and facilities!

The design of a training program is so much more complicated now, because we have a better understanding of the specific physiological adaptations that take place with a given form of training stimulus—the specificity of training principle. A well-designed program needs to consider each of the factors that determine performance in the water. How do we combine the methods described in the previous chapter, with their many variations, into the optimal training program, the program that will optimize performance? No one knows for sure. There is no secret formula that works for every individual in every situation. That's why coaching is part science and part art. The best we can do is provide a basic outline, founded on the principle of stress and adaptation, and trust each individual to exercise his or her own artistic license. Since each individual is different and responds differently to a training stimulus, he or she needs to recognize when it's necessary to apply more training stress and when it's necessary to back off.

Individual differences are especially important to consider when designing a training program for the older athlete. Even a very well trained 50-year-old swimmer would have a hard time handling the same volume of training as a college-age swimmer. This is due to the basic age-related physiological differences between a 20-year-old and a 50-year-old discussed previously. The over-50 athlete has less physical reserve capacity and less ability to adapt quickly. This means that the same training stress that produces desirable adaptations in the 20-year-old may result in exhaustion for the 50-year-old. The latter will need more recovery time before the next training stimulus. We need a plan that will program in periods of recovery.

Periodization

The idea of periodization of training was introduced to formalize variations in training intensity. The basic concepts associated with periodized training are not new. Doc Counsilman discussed periodization in his original 1968 *Science of Swimming*, but without all the macro/meso/micro mumbo-jumbo in use today. Doc broke the season into four phases: preseason, preparatory, hard-training, and taper. Within each phase were high-pressure and low-pressure workouts. The five types of training were combined to form an integrated workout. His system worked so well that the rest of the world copied it. Periodization schemes in use today are not much different from Doc's; only the nomenclature has changed. The most widely used terminology is detailed in *Theory and Methodology of Training* by Tudor Bompa, a challenging work to embrace, even for exercise physiologists. We'll present only those concepts of this complicated subject that will help us design a structured training program for the past-50 swimmer.

The central theme of periodized training is that optimal performance cannot be obtained by stressing the body with the same training stimulus day in and day out. Young athletes, high school swimmers for example, are implored by their coaches to "leave it in the pool" at every practice, *every day*. "No pain — No gain" is the mantra that is pounded into their heads. Some of them can take the punishment and survive, but many can't, so they switch to soccer or some other "play" sport. Even a young body cannot withstand hard work every day. It would spell disaster for the over-50 swimmer. The older body simply can't recover quickly enough to train hard every day. With periodized training, hard days are combined with easy days in a cyclic manner to allow recovery.

Rest is an important part of a periodized training plan.

Periodization is not as simple as alternating hard days with easy days, however. We need to have a weekly plan, a plan for the season, a plan for the year, and even a plan for the entire career, which for the past-50 swimmer is a lifetime plan. Let's start with long-term planning and work our way down to a single workout. An outline of the components of periodization is presented below.

Multiyear Cycle

At the highest level is the multiyear cycle. For the collegiate or Olympic athlete this would correspond to the four years of schooling or the time between Olympiads. For the fitness swimmer the multiyear cycle can be considered a lifelong cycle because the plan is to continue exercising for as long as possible. For the competitive Masters swimmer, however, the multiyear cycle is usually five years, the time span between successive age groups. If you are at the "bottom" of your age

---

CYCLES OF A PERIODIZED TRAINING PLAN FOR A PAST-50 SWIMMER

Multiyear Cycle (five years)
Every five years you "age up" into an older group
Annual Cycle (one year)
Consists of two macrocycles or seasons, winter and summer
Macrocycle (four to eight months)
Consists of three mesocycles, or training phases
Mesocycle (one to four months)
Consists of four to 16 microcycles
There are three types of mesocycle, each with a specific emphasis:
   Preparatory (General and Specific)
   Competitive (Precompetition, Main Competition, Taper)
   Transition
Microcycle (one week)
Consists of seven days of training
The emphasis of a given microcycle is dependent upon the type of mesocycle.
Workout (one or two per day)
The emphasis of a given workout is dependent upon its position within the microcycle: aerobic base, power, maintenance, or recovery.

group you are competing against people who are older than you, and you look forward to having a good year. The prospects for success motivate you to train harder, too. If you are at the "top" of your age group, you may back off in your training because you know you have the disadvantage of competing against younger people. Masters swimmers are perhaps the only adults who look forward to "aging-up!" Ginger Ladich Pierson describes her multiyear plan like this: "When planning for an age group change I start the initial buildup right in the middle of the age group, i.e., I'll start when I'm 53 and a half for March of the year I turn 55. I'll be doing 6 days a week, with two practices a day on 2 or 3 of those days." That's pretty serious training, but she only does it every five years, which makes it possible for her to focus so much energy into swimming. Ginger is following a multiyear cycle.

Macrocycle

Each year of a multiyear cycle contains several macrocycles, or seasons. In swimming we have two seasons per year, and

This past-50 swimmer is training during the summer macrocycle.

GINGER LADICH PIERSON

Home: Portland, Oregon
Current age group: 50 to 54
Started Masters swimming at age 36.

Ginger started age group swimming at the age of nine and continued until the age of 21. After a few years off she started competing again to prepare for the Ironman triathlon in 1982. She has also run the Portland Marathon. Ginger had the best race of her life in 1985 at age 39. Although she placed second, she broke the national record in the 200-yard breaststroke. Ten years later at age 49 she broke the world record in the short course meters 200 breaststroke.

Ginger swims four to six days a week, 4,000 to 5,500 yards. Her team has two coaches who plan all the workouts. She lifts weights three times a week for 45 minutes and stretches daily. During the off-season she runs, bikes, and does triathlon—all for cross-training. She also skis, but for pleasure only.

I currently don't have that "burning desire" to excel that I once had. However, I like to rise to a challenge, whether it's with Carolyn Boak or getting a high point award. I am somewhat blasé about competing, yet I'm more involved with tasks (processing entries, etc.). Because Masters swimming is really my extended family, I dread the passing or pain of my family members. On my journey through swimming I have met people from all over the world—an opportunity of enjoyment for a lifetime. It's not the destination that matters, but the journey.

Ginger describes her training program:

My year of training begins in September and is focused in three seasons. The *early or beginning season* (Sept–Jan) is devoted to cardiovascular emphasis, for example, repeat 800s and 1500s free or 300/400s stroke, as well as focusing on stroke technique. *Mid-season* (Feb-April) focuses on race strategy using broken sets of short interval attempting to achieve race pace times with as little effort as possible (distance per stroke). *Peak season* (May and August) provides long rest with quality swims of race length or even broken sets.

Warm-up varies in distance from 1000 to 15000 meters. Warm-down is occasionally in the form of quality drills (to leave a good "feel") but can be a straight easy swim. Variety in sets and regularity are considered to provide me a challenge as well as stimulation.

therefore two macrocycles, the winter short course (25 yards or meters) season and the summer, or outdoor (50 meters) season. Obviously these two macrocycles are not of the same length. The short course season runs from September or October to the middle of May, while the long course season comprises the summer months of June, July, and August.

Mesocycle

Each macrocycle is partitioned into three mesocycles that correspond to the following phases of the season:

- Preparatory
- Competitive
- Transition

The preparatory mesocycle is the time in the season when no competitions are held, and the training emphasis is on aerobic base and technique. The training emphasis during the initial months of the preparatory mesocycle is toward general preparation: over-distance, speed play, and slow interval training in all of the strokes, focusing on improving mechanics. The emphasis during the latter stage of the preparatory mesocycle shifts to specific preparation, with more quality work in the strokes to be used in competition.

The competitive mesocycle is further subdivided into three subphases. The initial two or three weeks are called the precompetitive phase and serve as a transition between the base training of the preparatory mesocycle and the higher quality training of the competitive mesocycle. The months during which one-day meets are held (January-April and June-July) constitute the main competitive phase. During this phase the emphasis of the workout plan is on attaining speed through fast interval training, goal sets, and sprints, but with enough moderate efforts to maintain an aerobic base. It is wise to reduce training stress a few days before each meet to give yourself a chance for a satisfactory performance. This brief rest from the usual grind is called unloading or peaking. A full taper, the final subphase of the competitive mesocycle, occurs only once per macrocycle, and can last as long as two weeks. During the taper, the emphasis is on rest and fine tuning in preparation for the championship meet. A common mistake is to wait until the taper to develop speed. By then it's too late. Speed is developed during the main competitive phase. By sprinting too much during a taper you'll come to the meet tired. As they say, you'll "leave your race in the workout." The most important aspect of the taper is rest. Rest is good!

The transition mesocycle follows the big meet and leads smoothly into the next macrocycle, the transition from short course to long course, for example. Many young athletes like to rest completely during the transition mesocycle—they do no form of exercise at all. This is a big mistake for the older athlete. It is much too hard to get going again. Again Ginger Ladich Pierson describes her program:

> I used to take a break for a month and a half after long course nationals when I was 36–38. It became harder and harder to get back into it (I ached, became nauseated, couldn't sleep, etc.). I decided that this really was a lifetime fitness program so I "swim around" with different environments for my break—outdoors, open water, different teams, etc.—but no pressure.

Cross-training, which can be defined as using multiple activities to achieve total body fitness, is often mentioned as a good way to stay in shape during the transition mesocycle. Running and biking can maintain the central (heart and lung) adaptations gained in the pool, but they will do little to retain the swimming-specific peripheral (muscle) effects of training. The transition mesocycle may be a good time to put more emphasis on dryland strength training.

Microcycle

Finally, each mesocycle (preparatory, competition, transition) consists of several microcycles, which usually correspond to one week. For example, the four-month competitive mesocycle (January to April) is divided into 16 microcycles, each with its own training emphasis. The microcycle, defined as one week for convenience only, corresponds to the workweek. There is no physiological significance to a seven-day microcycle. In fact, a shorter or longer cycle may be more appropriate for some swimmers. The purpose of a microcycle is to plan the optimal combination of intensity, volume, and rest. The characteristics of a given microcycle depend on the mesocycle and macrocycle within which it occurs. For example, a microcycle in the preparatory mesocycle of the winter macrocycle may be different from a microcycle in the competitive mesocycle of the summer macrocycle. The first microcycle will emphasize aerobic base, while the second will include more speed training.

A microcycle is broken down into the smallest unit of the training plan, an individual workout. Each workout should have a purpose, a goal within the overall training plan. We can classify a workout by the amount of stress, which is defined as a combination of training volume and intensity, that the session places on the body. If maximum stress is considered to be 100 percent, then the classifications are heavy (90–100 percent), medium (80–90 percent), light (50–80 percent), and recovery (no stress). We can define four goals for a given workout in the microcycle:

- Aerobic base
- Power
- Maintenance
- Recovery

An **aerobic base** workout emphasizes over-distance, speed play, or slow interval training with short rest at moderate intensity. It is classified as moderate to light in stress. A **power** workout may include some sprinting and a goal set or fast interval training (long rest, high intensity). Other terminology used to describe a power workout include anaerobic training and lactate training. No matter what you call it, power training is heavy stress and therefore very fatiguing. It should not be employed too often, no more than once or twice per microcycle. **Maintenance** workouts are those in which you get wet but stress is minimized—light stress. Maintenance days are especially important to the past-50 swimmer in order to allow recovery from higher stress workouts, without losing the physiological adaptations gained. It is much easier to maintain these adaptations than it was to attain them in the first place. Examples of low-stress work include moderate swimming trying to achieve "technical perfection," swimming with fins, stroke drills, and swimming your "off" strokes. Maintenance days are good for emphasizing technique. **Recovery** days are days off, no training, and may be absolutely essential for some older athletes who need more rest between hard efforts to prevent failing adaptation. An example of how these four goals might fit together into a seven-day microcycle is presented below.

Workout Structure

The structure of an individual workout also follows a plan. The basic structure is as follows:

- Introduction
- Warm-up
- Main set or sets
- Conclusion

EXAMPLE OF A MICROCYCLE WITHIN A PERIODIZED TRAINING PLAN

Day 1: Aerobic base (over-distance)
Day 2: Power (fast intervals, sprints)
Day 3: Maintenance (work on technique)
Day 4: Recovery (day off)
Day 5: Aerobic base (slow intervals, speed play)
Day 6: Specific speed (goal set)
Day 7: Recovery (day off)

The **introduction** consists of all the activities that take place before getting wet, such as stretching, getting workout instructions from the coach, and socializing. The **warm-up** has two phases, a general phase that consists of long slow distance plus slow kicking and/or pulling, followed by a specific phase consisting of a warm-up set swum at low intensity with short rest. The general warm-up is a physiological warm-up to increase heart rate, blood flow, joint lubrication, and muscle temperature. The specific warm-up, done as a low-quality set of swimming, kicking, or pulling, serves as a neurological warm-up to prepare the nerve pathways from the brain to the muscles for the intensity of the main set to follow.

There's an almost infinite number of ways to structure the **main set**. A workout may have more than one main set, separated by recovery swimming, kicking, or pulling. Each main set should have a specific physiological purpose based on the goal of the workout: aerobic base, power, or maintenance. More than one main set adds variety to the workout because each main set may have a different purpose. Combining several different training methods into a single workout in this manner to achieve more than one training goal results in an integrated or mixed workout structure. The combinations are almost limitless, which allows for tremendous variety in workout planning. But, variety for variety's sake defeats the goal of assigning a purpose to each part of the workout, unless, of course, the sole purpose of the set *is* variety.

The **conclusion** can be a sprint set or start and turn practice, followed by easy swimming. More than merely a physiological cooldown, it should serve as a transition from the intensity of the main set to the pleasure of the shower room, giving people a chance to wind down before returning to the real world.

An example of a workout will illustrate these points. Let's analyze the following training session.

> Warm-up 400 swim, 200 kick, 200 pull
> Swim 8 × 50 on 1:00, descend 1-4, 5-8
> Swim 10 × 100 on 2:00, hold a steady pace
> Swim 4 × 25 sprints
> Swim 200 easy

A well-designed workout provides motivation, and is more enjoyable than training on your own.

This 2,500-yard workout would be classified as aerobic base because the main set, 10 × 100 on 2:00, is an interval set that trains the aerobic system. The workout starts off with a general warm-up of swimming, kicking, and pulling. The intensity is very low, because the purpose is to loosen up the body. The general warm-up is followed by a specific warm-up of 8 × 50 on 1:00. This is supposed to be an easy set. The purpose is to *gently* increase intensity in preparation for the main set. The rest interval should be set so at least 10 seconds of rest are available between repeats. Add time to the interval if necessary. Descend 1-4, 5-8 means the intensity should increase from slow to fast from the first 50 to the fourth. The fifth 50 is easy again, descending again to fast on the eighth 50. By the end of this set you should be revved up for the main set. The main set is the meat of the workout. Ideally you should hold the same pace, hit the same time, on all 10 of the 100s. The rest interval is not very long, so your heart rate will stay fairly high throughout the 20 minutes it takes to complete the set. This is excellent aerobic training. Add time to the interval if you aren't getting at least 30 seconds of rest between repeats. Following the main set is the conclusion, which in this case consists of a few sprints and a cooldown. Sprints are important throughout the year to maintain fast-twitch fibers. This workout can be completed by most past-50 swimmers in about an hour, depending on skill level and how much time you rest between sets.

A workout can be as complicated or as simple as you like, as long as the desired training stimuli are present. The basic plan presented above is an example of an integrated workout structure. Each part of the workout should have a specific purpose, planned ahead of time. The details of each part of the workout (rest intervals, strokes, etc.) depend on many factors, including the cycle of the training plan, the skill and fitness level of the swimmer, and the events for which the swimmer is training. With so many variables involved it is necessary to put the plan on paper. By writing out the workout in advance you avoid what we call the "how about" workout. Before getting in the water someone says "how about warming up 500." At the conclusion of the warm-up, someone else says "how about doing 10 × 50 on one minute," etc. This isn't the way to design a good training program. A written plan helps assure continuity and organization from day to day. If you are going to spend so much time and energy in the pool, you may as well spend it wisely so that you reap optimal benefit from your efforts. Several examples of mixed workouts that follow this general plan are presented in chapter 9.

Training Volume

How much do past-50 swimmers train? Researchers at the Indiana University Human Performance Lab asked this question of the participants at the 1998 USMS short course national championships in Indianapolis. What they told us is presented in table 4.1, separated into those under 65 and those 65 and over. Our sample of Masters swimmers trains about four days per week, eleven months out of the year, with those 65 and over doing fewer yards per day than those under 65. It's interesting that the average distance per workout, 2,100 to 2,800 yards, fits comfortably into a one-hour block of

Table 4.1

SUMMARY OF USMS TRAINING SURVEY

	AGE GROUP	
	50 to 64	**65 to 96**
Number of swimmers	79	44
Swimming, yards/day	2,800	2,100
Swimming, days/week	4.2	4.2
Swimming, months/year	10.8	11.1
Other activity, hours/week	4.4	7.0
Age at first swimming meet	21	26
Age at first Masters meet	42	53

time for most swimmers of the skill level seen at the national championships. There were no differences in volume of swim training between men and women. As expected, the men started swimming competitively at an earlier age, especially in the over-65 group, due to the absence of competitive opportunities for women in the 1930s and '40s.

The surprising result from the study was the difference in the amount of time devoted to other fitness activities. Although the older age group swam fewer yards per week, they spent over two and a half hours more per week than the younger group on other activities, presumably because most people over 65 are retired. The women in both age groups spent considerably more time on other activities than the men. Clearly all these swimmers are "abnormal" when compared to the average sedentary American of any age. Our congratulations to them on their "abnormality"!

Training While Traveling

Serious swim training and frequent traveling do not make a good combination. The key to athletic success for the older swimmer is consistency, and it's difficult to be consistent and follow a structured training plan if you are on the road a lot. Young swimmers can take a few days or a week off and return to the pool without losing very much. However, for the 60-year-

International Stock/Scott Barrow

This past-50 swimmer enjoys training at least four days each week.

old, a week with no exercise seems like a lifetime, and it will feel like you're starting from scratch. In reality, fitness returns to normal fairly quickly after a *short* layoff. So how can you maintain your conditioning when business or vacation travel forces you to miss workouts?

A few years ago it would have been nearly impossible, but today, because of the proliferation of aquatic facilities and increased pool hours, swimming can now be a viable form of regular exercise for the frequent traveler. Ideally, you may be able to find a local YMCA or Masters swimming group with lap swimming times or organized practices that fit your schedule. How do you find these places? The *Swimmers Guide: Directory of Pools for Fitness Swimmers*, available in bookstores, contains listings for 3,000 pools throughout the country, with location, facilities, cost, and contact information. This book could be invaluable to the frequent traveler. For those wishing to find an organized workout, the National Office of United

States Masters Swimming (USMS) sells a *Places to Swim* publication that lists contact information for local Masters swim clubs. Those with World Wide Web access can view it for free at www.usms.org. An e-mail or phone call can put you in touch with someone who will help you arrange workout times. Please note that for insurance purposes, all swimmers in a USMS-sanctioned workout are required to be registered USMS members. Most teams are more than happy to have you join them for a few days, and invariably, the change in environment, workout style, and people serve as a refreshing change of pace.

However, if you cannot find a local Masters group and you still want to work out, you'll be stuck with the pool available in your hotel. If you've ever tried to do a real workout in one of those 10-yard oval hotel pools, you know this isn't a truly viable option. These pools were designed for playing, not working. If size and shape weren't impediment enough, they usually feature a rope across the middle, cutting these pools in half! An option some people employ is to bring along a swim tether made of a four- to eight-foot length of surgical tubing and a web belt that allow you to swim tethered to the side of the pool. Swimming in place, however, is not conducive to good stroke mechanics. You tend to change your usual stroke pattern to compensate for the absence of moving water. Also, if you've ever swum in place like this for any length of time, you know how absolutely mind-numbing it can be. Some hotels have a fairly decent size pool, but seldom do they offer the finer accoutrements, such as lane lines, kickboards, or pace clocks. Beware of the hotel that advertises an "Olympic Size Pool." Hotel management obviously doesn't understand how big a 50-meter pool really is. There are very few hotels in the world that can afford to dedicate that much space, and you certainly won't find one in the middle of a big city.

A facility you will find in most modern hotels today, however, is a gym with exercise machines and weights. If you normally have difficulty fitting weights into your training routine, why not make your travel days a time to concentrate on your dryland program? You can get a cardiovascular workout on the exercise bike, treadmill, or stair stepper, do your usual resistance exercises with weights or surgical tubing, and use the pool in the way it was designed to be used, to relax. Because you won't be stressed from completing a predetermined number of yards, you can use the time to work on technical perfection by practicing streamlining and stroke drills, which is certainly more relaxing than doing a goal set! Since these pools tend to be fairly short, it's sometimes possible to cover the entire length underwater from a push-off if you streamline effectively. Make a game out of it. Work on your underwater dolphin kick and long breaststroke pullout, too. You just might be able to get some benefit out of that business trip after all.

chapter

5

Dryland Training

One of the most enjoyable aspects of swimming is the feeling of being surrounded and supported by water. You may be perfectly content to limit your involvement in the sport to water activities without dedicating precious time to dryland training. You may not perceive an exercise that does not involve water to be beneficial to your swimming performance. In reality, the evidence strongly supports the opposite viewpoint. In order for the older athlete to achieve peak performance in the water, some form of dryland training is absolutely essential, whether it be to prevent injury, improve strength, or increase range of motion. If you are really serious about reaching your potential as a swimmer, the best thing you can do is to dedicate a couple of hours per week to dryland training.

As you saw in chapter 2, muscle mass and flexibility in the joints decline with age. Briefly, aging results in a decrease in the force a muscle can generate, the speed with which it contracts, its ability to relax, and its ability to keep contracting (endurance). Muscles of the lower body decline faster than muscles of the upper body. Although strength is maintained fairly well up to the age of 60, it falls precipitously thereafter. Fortunately for the past-50 swimmer, this decline appears to be due more to disuse than to aging.

Muscles of any age respond spectacularly to regular resistive exercise. Strength gains in elderly subjects as high as 227 percent have been reported following training programs lasting just 12 weeks! In fact, resistance training programs have produced percentage increases in strength for older people, even as old as 96, that equal, and sometimes surpass, those seen in young people. Every swimmer over the age of 50 who is serious about performance should consider incorporating some form of strength training into his or her exercise program.

Some older swimmers avoid involvement in any kind of strength training program because they have been injured in the past or fear the possibility of injury due to lifting weights. We would like to take the opposite view and suggest that a properly designed strength training program is an excellent way of *preventing* injury.

Caution! Before attempting any of the exercises we describe, including flexibility exercises, warm up thoroughly. A good warm-up for a strength training session should include some form of aerobic exercise (swimming, biking, running, stair stepper, etc.) to elevate heart rate, raise body temperature, and increase blood flow to the muscles and joints. *Gently* swing the arms and move the legs through their entire range of motion to improve lubrication of the joint and stretch the muscles crossing it. ***Always begin any dryland training session gently!***

Strength Training to Prevent Injury

The process of regular swimming strengthens the "prime mover" muscles, those muscles that contribute to forward motion in the water. Look at any well-trained swimmer, and it's easy to see which muscles are the prime movers. They are the ones that are well developed, including the latissimus dorsi, pectoralis major, teres major, and triceps for the upper body and the quadriceps, gastrocnemius, and gluteals in the lower body (see figure 5.1). Later in this chapter, we'll suggest some dryland exercises to strengthen these muscles.

There are several smaller muscle groups, often ignored because they are not prime movers, that are crucial in maintaining the stability of joints. The shoulder joint is the least stable of the body, held together by an array of ligaments and muscles. The ligamentous structure provides little restraint to movement. This is good because it allows the mobility to do wonderful things with the arms, but it also increases the shoulder's susceptibility to injury. The stability muscles of the shoulder are not very glamorous because they're covered by larger muscles and therefore aren't visible from the outside. Nonetheless, they're extremely important to the shoulder. They're called shoulder stabilizers because they hold the head of the humerus and the glenoid together to keep the joint stable. Shoulder stabilizers include the rotator cuff muscles: supraspinatus, infraspinatus, teres minor, and subscapularis (SITS muscles), plus the rhomboids and deltoids. As the prime movers become stronger through swimming, they can overpower the ability of the shoulder stabilizers to maintain proper shoulder alignment. The result is the poor posture so characteristic of swimmers—slumped shoulders pulled forward by the pectoralis major and a curved back. Poor alignment can lead to impingement of the shoulder tendons and the development of the tendinitis that so many swimmers suffer, a condition so prevalent that it has its own name in the medical literature—"Swimmer's Shoulder."

The preventative solution to swimmer's shoulder is to strengthen the shoulder stabilizer muscles in order to maintain proper alignment. Unfortunately, swimming does little to strengthen these muscles. You must do some form of dryland exercising specifically designed to isolate them. We'll now describe these exercises and indicate the muscles they are designed to strengthen. Some of the exercises described can be found in an excellent article by Dr. John Aronen that appeared in the April 1985 issue of *Swimming World*. Others were supplied by Stephanie Janssen, athletic trainer for aquatic sports at Indiana University. Only recently has attention been focused on the shoulder stabilizer exercises for the prevention of swimming injuries. It's possible that these exercises are completely new to most past-50 swimmers. Fortuitously, this is the group that should benefit the most from doing them, given that years and years of training can create serious muscle imbalances, resulting in shoulder instability.

The following exercises are intended to be done with surgical tubing, which can be purchased by the foot at a medical supply store. Besides being economical, surgical tubing is lightweight, portable, and waterproof, and therefore travels well

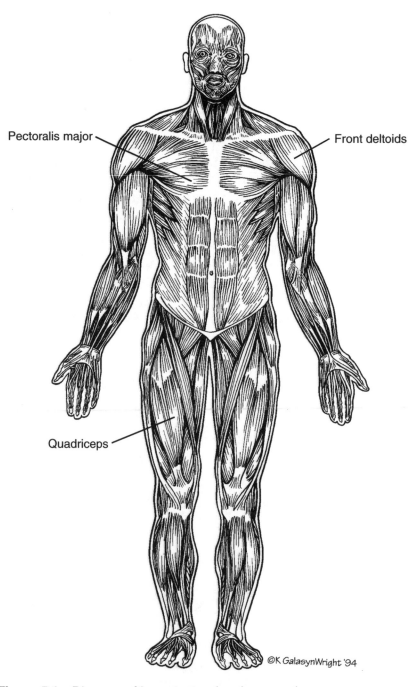

Pectoralis major

Front deltoids

Quadriceps

©K GalasynWright '94

Figure 5.1 Diagram of important swimming muscles.

© K. Galasyn-Wright, Champaign, IL, 1994.

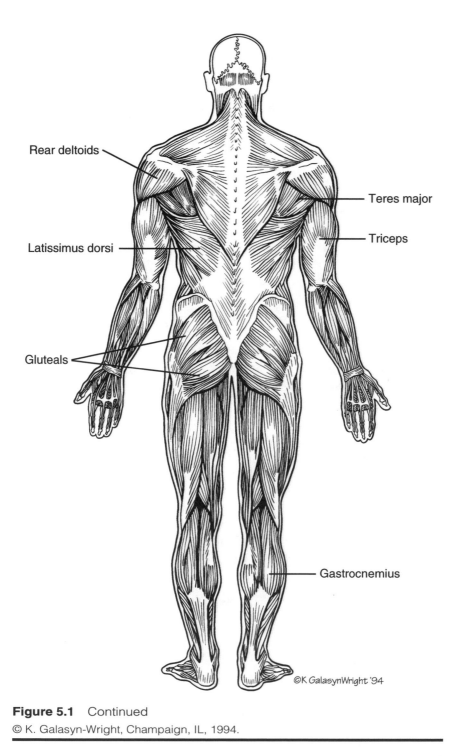

Rear deltoids

Latissimus dorsi

Gluteals

Teres major

Triceps

Gastrocnemius

©K GalasynWright '94

Figure 5.1 Continued
© K. Galasyn-Wright, Champaign, IL, 1994.

with you to the pool. Tubing comes in a variety of resistances determined by the size. The recommended inside diameter is 3/16 inch with a 3/32-inch wall thickness, about five feet long. You can vary the tension by changing the length of the tubing, shorter tubing will provide greater resistance. In place of tubing, you can use light weights, starting with one pound and working your way up. Even common household items such as a jar of peanut butter, a can of soup, or a milk jug full of water can serve as resistance. An old bicycle tube, cut to make one six-foot length, may also work well. You don't need expensive, heavy, or large equipment to give yourself an effective strength-training workout.

Even though these exercises do not appear to be very strenuous, they are still beneficial. Doing them should not be painful. In this case no pain *is* gain. If you've never trained the shoulder stabilizers before, your gain will be noticeable right away. Since most of these muscles are small, it doesn't take much resistance to fatigue them, nor does it take much resistance to strengthen them. Start with very little or no tension, two sets of 10 repetitions on each arm, then increase tension and/or repetitions as strength improves. The correct form is demonstrated in figures 5.2 through 5.7. Make sure you don't shrug your shoulders while doing the surgical tubing exercises. If your neck is tired after exercising you haven't done them properly. When possible, perform the exercises with both arms together, which promotes the correct symmetrical form and eliminates the chances of cheating by leaning away from the cord.

Avoid any of the following exercises if they cause pain due to existing injuries. A qualified physical therapist should be consulted in order to rehabilitate existing injuries.

• *Anterior deltoid exercise:* Hold one end of the tubing in your right hand and place the other end under your right foot to the desired tension. Assuming that the 12:00 position is straight ahead, start with the arm in the 1:00 position, thumb up, elbow straight, and stretch the tubing until the arm reaches shoulder level. Relax and repeat for a total of 10 reps. Switch to the left arm and start from the 11:00 position (figure 5.2).

Figure 5.2 Anterior deltoid exercise.

• *Supraspinatus exercise:* Assume the same initial position as described above but with the arm toward the 2:00 direction. Point the thumb downward in what is called the "empty can" position, so named because this is the way you would hold your hand to empty a can. This position of the arm and hand is necessary to isolate the supraspinatus muscle. Lift your arms to about 45 degrees only (figure 5.3).

Figure 5.3   Supraspinatus exercise.

• *Middle deltoid exercise:* Assume the same initial position but start with the arm at the 3:00 position with the back of the hand straight up (figure 5.4). Raise vertically as shown.

Figure 5.4 Middle deltoid exercise.

• *Posterior deltoid exercise:* Start with the arm behind you at the 5:00 position and the thumb pointing down (figure 5.5). Raise vertically as shown.

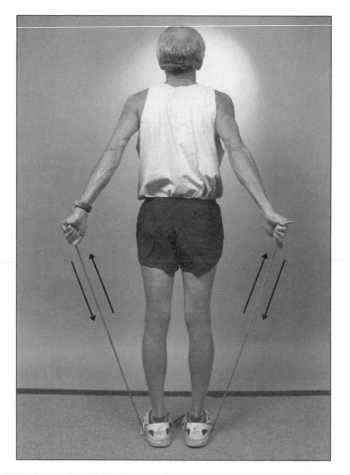

Figure 5.5 Posterior deltoid exercise.

• *Internal rotation exercise:* Secure the free end of the tubing to a door knob or other immovable structure at hip height. With the elbow bent 90 degrees and the arm pointing in the 3:00 position, internally rotate the shoulder across the body to the 10:00 position. Keep the elbow against the side throughout the movement. This exercise strengthens the internal rotators of the rotator cuff (figure 5.6).

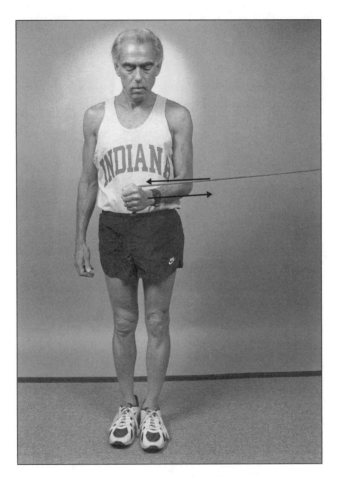

Figure 5.6   Internal rotation exercise.

• *External rotation exercise:* Turn and face the other direction so the tubing resists external rotation to strengthen the external rotators of the rotator cuff. Again, keep the elbow against the side and rotate across the body from the 10:00 position to the 3:00 position. Perform the movement with the arms only, with no twisting of the hips and trunk (figure 5.7).

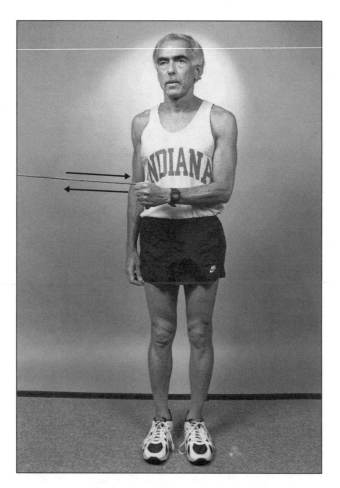

Figure 5.7   External rotation exercise.

• *Rowing exercise:* This exercise is for scapular stabilization and should be done lying face down on a table with the arm dangling over the side. Lift a weight in a rowing motion with the arm at 90 degrees to the body.

• *Push-up with a "plus" motion:* This exercise is also for scapular stabilization and strengthens the serratus anterior. At the end of a normal push-up, perform an extra push to protract the scapula and round the back. If a normal push-up is too difficult, this exercise can be performed standing up by leaning against a wall. The important movement is the protraction of the scapula.

These eight exercises aren't very strenuous and don't take very much time, but they can be the most valuable exercises a past-50 swimmer can do to prevent shoulder injury. If you are reluctant to try a weightlifting program for fear of injury, consider trying these simple exercises. Stronger shoulder stabilizer muscles may not make you swim faster, but they will certainly make your shoulders feel more stable, which may allow you to increase the strength of the prime mover muscles.

Strength Training to Swim Faster

As we've noted, swimming is a *power* sport. The best swimmers are those who can generate a large force (strength) very quickly (speed). Strength and speed together define power. Studies have shown that power correlates most highly with swim performance, more so than strength or flexibility. How can we develop power? We can create a larger force by improving strength, or we can move more quickly. The older athlete, however, has a problem. The muscle fibers that generate the greatest force and are best suited for making quick movements are the fast-twitch (Type IIa and IIb) fibers. Unfortunately, these are the fibers that have been shown to be preferentially lost via atrophy as the muscle ages. Older individuals in general have a higher percentage of slow-twitch muscle fibers than young people. It is still not clear whether this difference is due to aging or the simple fact that older individuals do not use their fast-twitch fibers, resulting in their atrophy. If you want to keep them, you'll need to use them.

There are two ways you can recruit your fast-twitch fibers. You can swim very fast in the pool, thereby requiring your muscles to generate the kind of forces that recruit fast-twitch fibers, or you can overload your muscles by performing dryland resistance exercises. The former option is often the least popular. Many past-50 swimmers suffer from a condition that prevents them from recruiting their fast-twitch fibers in the pool. We call it yardage mania. Here's how it works. With a limited amount of time to devote to daily exercise, they want to make the best of it. Since our culture has ingrained in us the notion "more is better," they go to the pool with the goal of getting in as much yardage as possible. This usually means their workout will consist of moderate efforts with very little rest. If the rest interval is too long, they won't achieve their yardage goal for the day in the allotted time. This is great training for their slow-twitch fibers but doesn't do much for the fast ones. Obviously, the all-out efforts that are needed to recruit fast-twitch fibers will require more rest between repeats. The yardage mania sufferer sees this as a waste of valuable time since his or her daily yardage goal is perceived as being more important. A second factor that prevents many past-50 swimmers from recruiting their fast-twitch fibers in practice is pain. Maximal efforts aren't very pleasant. The result is that goal sets and all-out sprints with long rest tend to get left out of the training plan. When the meet rolls around, the poor fast-twitch fibers, those that are left, pay a big price because they're asked to do something they weren't trained to do—swim fast! Clearly, yardage mania prevents many past-50 swimmers from reaching their true potential as athletes.

The solution to this problem is to hit the weight room. No other dryland activity will benefit your swimming performance more than a regular program of resistance training. Your fast-twitch fibers will thank you for your efforts at the next meet. Notice that we say *resistance* training and not *weight* training. There are many ways to build strength. You don't need to lift the huge weights pictured in the muscle magazines. In fact, lifting heavy weights isn't recommended for older swimmers. Instead, we recommend lighter weights, dumbbells, machines, and elastic tubing. It doesn't take very much resistance training to feel an increase in strength, especially in muscles that haven't been exercised in this way before. Age isn't a factor in the response of muscle to training. Ninety-year-old muscles respond just as readily to resistance training as do 25-year-old muscles.

Basic Principles of Resistance Training

The basic principles of resistance training are so obvious you won't believe you didn't think of them yourself. First is the principle of specificity of training, which states that the body makes specific adaptations to specific types of training. Therefore, you should design your training to be *specific* to your sport, in this case swimming. The principle of progressive overload states that in order for a training stimulus to be effective it must stress the body, or parts of the body, to levels above those normally experienced. Furthermore, the stimulus must gradually increase in a systematic manner. Therefore, according to these principles, you can improve your swimming performance by progressively overloading your muscles with resistance exercises that are specific to swimming. In theory it sounds simple. In practice, it is! We guarantee that the results are worth the effort.

Strength Versus Endurance

Swimming is a difficult sport for which to strength train because the events range in duration from 30 seconds to one hour or more. Participants don't specialize by event the way track athletes do. Can you imagine a 100-meter track sprinter running in a marathon? Swimmers, however, especially swimmers in the higher age groups who are searching for new challenges, enjoy sampling the entire spectrum of events. They want to swim the 50 free and the 5K, and they want to perform well in both. You need strength to improve power for the 50, and you need endurance for the 5K.

What type of resistance training should you do? Is it better to do high repetitions with a light weight or use a heavier weight and do fewer repetitions? We need to apply the principle of specificity of training to this problem. It takes the form of DeLorme's Principle of resistance training, which states that in order to develop strength, the training stimulus should consist of high resistance (heavy weights) and low repetitions, while to develop endurance use low resistance with high

NANCY RIDOUT

Home: Novato, California
Current age group: 55 to 59
Started Masters swimming at age 30.

Nancy competed in swimming in her youth and continued during her college years, although there was no collegiate swimming for women at the time (1960–64). During high school and college she also competed in several other sports, including water polo, synchronized swimming, kayaking, war canoe, field hockey, and gymnastics. In 1972 she started Masters swimming. Her biggest thrill came four years later when she broke a minute in the 100-yard freestyle for the first time. "It had been a lifelong goal from my youth, long abandoned, which I never dreamed I would attain." She did even better at the age of 42, clocking 58.2 in the 100.

Courtesy of Nancy Ridout

At the Short Course Nationals in 1996, in Cupertino, CA, age 54, I experienced not only satisfaction but an inner sense of renewal again as a swimmer. The year before had been particularly depressing. My racing and training went downhill from age 51–53 and I was very discouraged. After I began resistance, flexibility, and range of motion training, my swimming career turned around 180 degrees. The times, training, and overall fitness I achieved at age 54 were as personally rewarding and satisfying to me as any other.

They were a surprise to other swimmers as well! Nancy used to train a lot more yardage than she does today. When she turned 45 she decided to train 3,500 rather than 4,500 a workout. She hoped that would be sufficient because she wanted to have enough energy to "smell the roses" for the remainder of her life. Now she trains 3,000 to 3,500, sometimes more when she's getting a base for the Hour Swim. A favorite workout would not include long swims. It's not the distance (she doesn't mind 20 × 100 or 6–8 × 200), she just doesn't like swimming in a pool for a long distance as a rule.

First of all, I have always considered myself a sprinter. When the concept of the Hour Swim came up, in 1977, my coach thought we should participate. I was not at all sure I could do it, but I tried and succeeded. I have never liked or enjoyed that event, but there is a certain amount of satisfaction in meeting a challenge. I experienced just as much apprehension and dread at age 56 as I did that first time.

Nancy, who is currently the president of United States Masters Swimming, explains how swimming affects her life:

Swimming gives my life breadth and depth. It keeps my body fit and allows my soul to sing. It has brought me new friends and has given me long and rich relationships. Swimming has afforded me the opportunity to give as well as receive. Swimming is an integral part of my life. It makes me feel whole.

Nancy's Sample Workout

Warm-up: 400 swim, 200 kick, 200 pull

Swim 3 × 100 Drills

Nancy likes to work on two or three things, then put it all together on the fourth lap. For example, each 25 emphasize catch, leading with the shoulder, hip roll, then all of the above. Or 25 fists, 25 regular 3 2. Or, kick, right arm, left arm, build-up.

Main Set: Swim 10 × 100
  1–3 build-up on 1:30
  4–6 same time on 1:25
  7–9 descend on 1:30
  10 on 2 minutes—sprint
Swim 50 easy
Kick 6 × 50 on 1:00, trying to hold 50 seconds or better
  If over 50 for two consecutive 50s, add 5–10 second recovery and continue as before.
Swim 50 easy
Pull 3 × 200 moderate pace, 20 seconds rest
  Emphasize catch, pull-through, hip rotation, and streamlining.
Swim 100 easy warm-down
Total: 3,200 yards

repetitions. This principle suggests that you can't train optimally for strength and endurance at the same time. Just as in the pool you can't be at your peak for a 50 and a 5K on the same day, you must make a choice in the weight room—strength or endurance. Having presented you with that choice, we should also state that if you haven't lifted weights for many years, or have never touched a weight in your life, any type of resistance training will improve your strength, and the improvement will be very rapid. This is because initial gains in strength are a result of improved neuromuscular function and nerves adapt very quickly. This improved neuromuscular function will translate into improved performance in the water. You'll be better able to recruit the fast-twitch fibers that lay dormant before you called them back to life in the weight room. Muscle hypertrophy, an increase in muscle size, usually takes several weeks of serious training to become evident, and will be minimal in most older swimmers, despite a pronounced increase in strength. Keep in mind you're in the weight room as a means to an end, not an end in itself. You don't want to look like a model for one of the muscle magazines and shouldn't train like they do.

The resistance training program described below will emphasize endurance, doing high repetitions with low resistance, with the understanding that any type of resistance training will improve strength to some extent in people who never have lifted before. After consistently and safely following an endurance-type training program for several months without any injuries, you probably will reach a plateau in strength. If you wish to gain further increases in strength, you will need to apply DeLorme's Principle again and increase resistance while decreasing the number of repetitions, possibly incorporating the more explosive movements of the Olympic lifts. An excellent reference for this next step is *Strength Training Past 50* by Wayne Westcott and Thomas Baechle. The descriptions for the swimming exercises listed below are from chapter 5 of their book.

Exercises Specific to Swimming

In order to propose the resistance exercises that would be most specific to swimming we need to identify again the prime mover muscles. They are the latissimus dorsi, pectoralis major, teres major, and triceps in the upper body and the quadriceps, gastrocnemius, and gluteals in the lower body. Exercises that stress these muscles should translate into improved performance in the water. Every weight room has its own set of equipment—barbells, dumbbells, and assorted machines. *For your own safety, we recommend you ask the management of the facility where you plan to train to instruct you in the proper use of the equipment.* Here's a brief summary of exercises most beneficial for swimming and how to do them.

1. Lat Pull (machine)

Muscles: Latissimus dorsi, posterior deltoid

Grip the bar as wide as possible and bring it down behind the neck. Keep the trunk upright, without leaning the trunk or neck forward. Lat pulls may also may be performed by pulling the bar in front of the face to the upper chest.

2. Triceps Extension (dumbbell)

Muscles: Triceps

There are several ways to do triceps extension. Choose the one that best mimics the actions of your stroke. Here's an example. Grasp one dumbbell with both hands and stand erect. Lift dumbbell upward until arms are fully extended, directly above head. Keep upper arms perpendicular to floor throughout exercise. Slowly lower dumbbell toward base of neck. Lift dumbbell upward slowly until arms are fully extended again.

3. Biceps Curl (barbell or dumbbell)

Muscles: Biceps, brachialis

Although the biceps are not prime mover muscles in swimming it is important to strengthen them to maintain a balance with the triceps. Grasp bar or dumbbell with underhand grip, elbows slightly flexed. Keep torso erect. Slowly curl forearms upward until elbows are fully flexed. Keep wrists straight. Lower slowly to starting position.

4. Military Press or Shoulder Press (machine)

Muscles: Deltoids, upper trapezius, triceps

Grasp bar at shoulder height with palms turned forward. Slowly push upward until arms are fully extended over the shoulders. Keep head and back straight. Slowly lower to shoulder height. If the exercise is done with the bar behind the head, the middle and posterior deltoid, upper and middle trapezius, and the triceps will be included.

5. Bench Press (machine or barbell)

Muscles: Pectoralis major and minor, sternocleidomastoid, scalenus anterior

Grasp bar, hands slightly outside of shoulder width, with bar extending across the breast area. Push upward until arms are fully extended above chest. Keep head, shoulders, and buttocks in contact with the bench. In order to prevent harmful arching of the back, place feet on the bench rather than on the floor.

6. Rowing (machine)

Muscles: trapezius, rhomboids, deltoids, biceps, brachialis

This exercise is important for shoulder stability and to balance the development of the chest muscles. Grasp bar, arms fully extended. Slowly pull bar toward chest. Keep wrists straight. Be sure to squeeze shoulder blades together. Allow bar to return slowly until arms are fully extended.

7. Squat (dumbbells)

Muscles: Quadriceps (rectus femoris, lateralis, medialis, and intermedius)

Grasp dumbbells using an underhand grip and stand erect with feet about hip-width apart and parallel to each other. Keep head up, eyes fixed straight ahead, shoulders back, back straight, and weight on entire foot throughout the downward and upward movement phases. Slowly squat until thighs are parallel to floor. An alternative to the squat is the step-up. Hold dumbbells in hands and step up onto an aerobics bench, then back down, one leg at a time. Increase the height of the bench as you improve.

8. Crunches

Muscles: Rectus abdominus

There are literally dozens of ways to do abdominal exercises. Here's one: Lie on back, knees flexed, feet flat on floor. Place hands loosely behind head to maintain neutral neck position. Slowly raise shoulders about 30 degrees off floor. Slowly lower shoulders to floor.

There are many other exercises you can do, but these eight cover the prime mover muscles and a few others that are important for muscle balance. Again, consult your gym management for proper instruction on how to do these exercises with the available equipment.

The Four Rs of Exercise

There are four factors to consider when designing a resistance training program, the four Rs of exercise.

- Repetitions (How many sets and reps?)
- Resistance (How much weight or load?)
- Rate (How fast?)
- Rest (How much rest between sets and exercises?)

These factors are determined by the goal of the training stimulus. Because the initial strength training program for a past-50 swimmer should be designed for endurance, the correct combination of Rs should be 1 set of 10 repetitions with a weight that can be managed fairly easily for all 10 reps. Perform each rep at a moderate speed, then take about a minute of rest between sets. This entire workout should take less than 30 minutes, from warm-up to cooldown. After a few weeks of lifting two or three times per week, the number of sets can be increased to two and eventually three. The number of reps can also can be increased to 12 or 15. As strength increases, 15 reps will become too easy, so add a small increment in weight and decrease the number of reps while maintaining the same rate and rest. Eventually, strength development will reach a plateau. It will take eight to twelve weeks, depending on consistency. This time frame fits conveniently into the preparatory phase of a yearly training program. Thereafter, the goal is maintenance, a task that is much easier than was gaining the strength in the first place. Muscle strength can be maintained during the maintenance phase as long as the weight load remains constant, even though the number of days per week, the number of sets, and the number of reps per set are reduced. It's time to enjoy your new strength in the pool!

Stretch Cords

One of the best dryland training toys ever invented are stretch cords. They are cheap, portable, simple to use, and simulate the butterfly and freestyle pulls almost exactly, a perfect application of the specificity of training principle. They are available in a variety of styles and strengths. Start with the lightest resistance and work your way up. Attach one end to a door knob or other immovable object, step back a few feet, grab the two handles, and pull (see Figure 5.8). To make it easier,

Figure 5.8   Stretch cords are an excellent way to build strength.

move closer. To make it harder, move farther away. It's safer to pull with both arms at the same time, as if you are swimming butterfly, rather than trying to simulate freestyle by alternating arms. The first part of the breaststroke pull is just like butterfly. Backstroke is probably not an option. Stretch cord training is also a valuable way to visualize correct stroke mechanics. You can watch yourself throughout the pull pattern.

A stretch cord workout can be designed just like a pool workout—a warm-up followed by interval sets. It doesn't take very many repetitions to get tired, however, so 10 minutes of butterfly intervals is enough for most people. With a little ingenuity you also can imitate many of the exercises you normally would do with weights and save yourself a trip to the gym. Stretch cords are also a convenient way to train while traveling.

Scheduling Your Strength Workout

When is the best time to schedule resistance training: before swimming or after? There isn't a single best answer to this question. Common sense suggests that the quality of a pool workout will be sacrificed following a tiring resistance session. However, performance in the weight room, not to mention motivation, will be affected by a hard workout in the pool. The choice comes down to personal preference and where you place your priorities within your overall training plan. Ideally, strength training sessions should be scheduled so as not to conflict with pool workouts, either at the opposite end of the day, or on a separate day entirely. For example, if you swim in the morning you could lift in the evening, or you could lift on a day that you do not swim at all. It wouldn't be wise, however, to let your desire to improve strength rob you of the obligatory day each week of complete rest that you need for recovery from both pool workouts and strength training sessions.

Strength training will have a noticeable effect on your swimming performance. Initially, you'll feel stronger in the water because of the improvement in neuromuscular function discussed earlier. After a few weeks of hard efforts in the weight room, accumulated fatigue may negatively affect how you feel in the pool. Stick with it! You're in the fatigue zone, but you'll come out of it when you take a few weeks away from strength training before the big meet.

Stretching for Flexibility

Flexibility is another aspect of swim training that often is sacrificed to yardage mania. Almost every past-50 swimmer has been heard to proclaim, "I should stretch more." You know stretching is beneficial and you want to fit it in, but it doesn't get done during practice because you don't want to take time away from swimming. Stretching is not viewed as being important enough to sacrifice yardage out of the workout. What a big mistake!

It should come as no surprise to anyone reading this book that flexibility declines with age. This loss begins as early as age 20. The usual question can be posed: Is the decline in flexibility due to the effects of aging or to a sedentary lifestyle? One way to find out is to start a regular flexibility program and see what happens. Such studies have been done and they are encouraging. It has been demonstrated that stretching and a progressive-resistance exercise program produce the same percentage of improvement in range of motion in elderly subjects (age 63 to 88 years) as in young subjects (15 to 19 years). However, the joints of the older subjects remained stiffer than the joints of the younger individuals.

Flexibility can be defined as the ability to move a joint throughout its full range of motion. Flexibility declines with age because the connective tissues of the body, the rope-like collagen fibers and the rubber-band-like elastin fibers, become stiffer and lose their ability to stretch. Poor flexibility increases the chance of injury. Exercise improves joint stability by increasing the strength of the tendons and muscles. Flexibility exercises improve the suppleness of tendons, ligaments, and muscles so that the joint can achieve its full range of motion.

Theories of Stretching

The most widely accepted theory of stretching is that described by Bob Anderson in his book, *Stretching*. According to this theory, stretching movements should be gentle and smooth, with no bouncing, and never to the point of pain. Breathing is slow, rhythmical, and under control. The correct technique involves two phases: the easy stretch and the developmental stretch. The easy stretch goes to the point of mild tension and is held from 10 to 30 seconds. The developmental stretch moves the joint a fraction of an inch farther and is held for 30 seconds. The keys are to always be in control, never bounce, and don't make it hurt. This is another example of the "no pain means more gain" principle. Partner stretches, so popular in swimming a few years ago, are definitely not advised. *You* must be in control of how much your joint is being moved. Only *you* will know how much is too much. Stretching is not a team sport!

A relatively new method of stretching known as "active-isolated stretching" is becoming very popular with elite athletes and is worth investigating because it has been especially effective with elderly people. The method is described in *The Whartons' Stretch Book* by Jim and Phil Wharton. The theory revolves around the stretch reflex mechanism of the muscle, a nerve reflex that responds to overstretching of a muscle by telling it to contract, thereby protecting it from injury. The active-isolated stretching method aims to avoid activating the stretch reflex by initiating the stretch with contraction of the muscle that opposes the muscle to be stretched (the antagonist) and by holding the stretch for a few seconds only. Here's how the method is described in their book:

1. Prepare to stretch one isolated muscle at a time.
2. Actively contract the muscle that is *opposite* the isolated muscle. The isolated muscle then will relax in preparation for its stretch.
3. Stretch it gently and quickly—hold the stretch for no more than two seconds.
4. Release the stretch before the muscle reacts to being stretched (by going into its protective contraction).
5. Do it again.

They recommend 10 repetitions of each stretch, just as if you were doing a set of resistance exercises. Contraction of the opposite muscle generates heat and improves blood flow to the body part being stretched, so that active-isolated stretching can serve as both warm-up and flexibility time.

Stretches for Swimmers

When's the best time to stretch? A warm muscle is easier to stretch, so after a workout is a good time, but you'll feel better in the water if you stretch before the workout as well. Most experts recommend stretching both before and after training. There are as many stretching exercises as there are directions in which the body can be bent. Anderson lists 13 exercises that are specific to swimming, while the Whartons describe 59 possibilities. We'll mention just a few of our favorite upper-body exercises, as illustrated in figures 5.9 to 5.14. They're all easy stretches and can be done at work or in public without attracting too much attention.

• *Front shoulder stretch:* Clasp the hands behind the back and raise the arms. You should feel this stretch in the front of your shoulders. A simple shoulder blade squeeze will give you the same feeling and is an effective stretch while seated in a chair at work (figure 5.9).

Figure 5.9   Front shoulder stretch.

• *Posterior cuff stretch:* Grasp the opposite elbow and gently pull your arm across your body (figure 5.10).

Figure 5.10   Posterior cuff stretch.

• *Triceps stretch:* Place the right hand behind the right shoulder. Pull back on the elbow with the left hand, relax, then pull the elbow behind the head (figure 5.11).

Figure 5.11 Triceps stretch.

• *Front shoulder doorway stretch:* Place the hands and forearms on either side of a narrow doorway and lean forward, keeping the head up. Repeat the exercise with hands at different heights. A corner also will work for this exercise. Keep the head in line with the neck, without letting the head hang in front of the shoulders (figure 5.12).

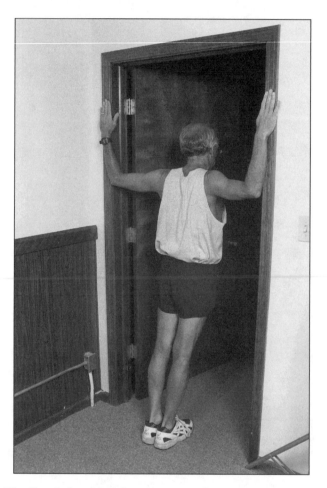

Figure 5.12 Front shoulder doorway stretch.

• *Rotator cuff stretch with arm overhead:* Use a door sill or overhead bar to gently stretch the arms backward above the head. Keep the head up as in the doorway stretch (figure 5.13).

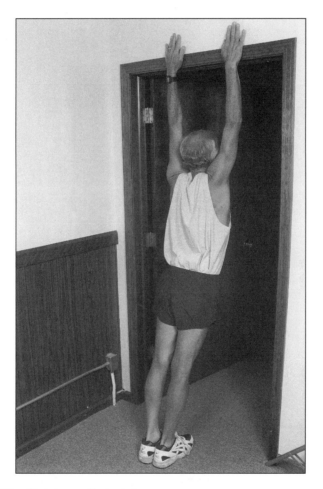

Figure 5.13 Rotator cuff stretch.

• *Bar hang:* Let gravity stretch your entire body while hanging from a bar (figure 5.14).

Figure 5.14 Bar hang stretch.

Dryland Training to Improve Performance

If your goal is to swim for the simple joy of being in the water then you probably don't need to do any type of dryland training. But if you want to improve your performance, then extra effort on strength and flexibility training is absolutely essential. The past-50 swimmer can't develop enough strength to reach his or her potential from swimming alone. Due to a relatively sedentary modern lifestyle, most adults have lost both strength and flexibility. It doesn't take very much time or effort in the weight room or gym to see an improvement in swimming performance, but it does require consistent attention to a regular program. The performance gain from even a minimal commitment to resistance exercises makes the time spent worthwhile. As an example of how beneficial a dryland program can be, Masters swimmer Nancy Ridout shares this story:

> For the past three years, my times had been falling off for no apparent reason. People told me I was getting older and not to fret (i.e., get used to it). I was almost ready to accept my new fate but decided to try weight training, which I had never done. Mark Stoker, a trainer in the fitness center, took an interest in me. Though not a swimmer himself, he was able to create a program that enhanced my strength for swimming. I worked hard in the pool and in the fitness center, under his direction, on resistance training, range of motion, and flexibility. At the Nationals in Cupertino, my 100-yard freestyle had improved three seconds; the 50, one second; and my 200 free, seven seconds from the year before—and I won all five events I swam! It meant a great deal to me to have been able to accomplish this and to share it with my husband and trainer, who were both present.

As Nancy's story illustrates, if your goal is to improve performance in the water, adding dryland training to your routine is a must.

chapter
6

Swimming Injuries: Prevention and Treatment

Swimming is a relatively injury-free sport, especially when compared with running. Nevertheless, injuries do occur. You may have been doing something you shouldn't have been doing, such as swimming hard without a warm-up, overexerting on a new exercise in the weight room, or stretching too far. Most swimming injuries, however, are some form of overuse syndrome: overuse of a tendon (tendinitis), overuse of a bursa (bursitis), or overstress of a muscle (strain). These injuries are all preventable and curable. The most common injury is to the shoulder—up to 60 percent of elite swimmers have had swimmer's shoulder at some time in their careers.

The prevalence of overuse injuries in past-50 swimmers is unknown, but by taking a few precautions the chances of injury while swimming can be minimized. The key is to stay within your physical capabilities, limits set by age, genetics, and previous training. Exceed those limits and you run the risk of failing adaptation, just like the mice in Dr. Selye's experiments. Something will fail—a muscle, a tendon, a joint, or your enthusiasm for swimming. One of the realities of aging is that it takes longer to recover from a stressful event, whether it be a hard workout, a minor injury, or an illness. The patience, or some would say the wisdom, to allow extra time for recovery is a trait that makes many past-50 swimmers so durable. Year after year they keep plugging away, with rarely a complaint. They know minor irritations can grow into major medical adventures if sufficient time isn't allowed to give their body a chance to recover.

Rest Is Good!

It may seem odd to start a chapter about injuries by discussing rest, but rest is the most often neglected aspect of exercise. There comes a time when the best form of training is rest. At the competitive level, it's often said that "while everyone knows how to train, winners know how to rest." For the past-50 swimmer, knowing how to rest can make the difference between staying healthy and missing days or weeks of exercise.

In chapter 4 we pointed out that the goal of a periodized training program is to plan periods of work carefully, followed by periods of recovery. A hard workout is supposed to make you tired. An easy workout or a day off allows you to recover. Several hard workouts in a row cause fatigue to accumulate so you feel tired at the next practice. This isn't a problem as long as you are adapting to the workload. You're in what Counsilman calls the fatigue zone, depicted graphically in figure 6.1. The solid line illustrates the theory of stress and adaptation. When you train optimally you enter the fatigue zone. Rest allows you to regain your energy and enter into the super adaptation zone. The theory of stress and adaptation holds that when you rest you'll regain your energy and enter into the adaptation zone. Your physical performance will be better than it was before you started this training cycle. Another cycle of fatigue and recovery raises your performance to an even higher level. If your training is not sufficiently intense to push deep enough into the fatigue zone, as illustrated by the upper dashed line, rest will only take you into the adaptation zone. Your performance

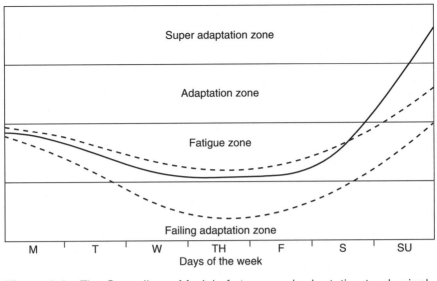

Figure 6.1   The Counsilman Model of stress and adaptation to physical loads.

From J. Counsilman and B. Counsilman, *The New Science of Swimming*.
Copyright © 1994. All rights reserved. Reprinted by permission of Allyn & Bacon.

will improve, but not as much as if you'd trained harder. The problem arises when fatigue piles on top of fatigue without sufficient recovery and your body is unable to adapt. You've pushed yourself into the failing adaptation zone, illustrated by the lower dashed line—the valley of fatigue. The consequence can be illness or injury. Your performance is worse than it was before you started training! This is why rest is such an important part of a training program.

How much rest does a past-50 swimmer need? It's difficult to answer that question, but the amount is certainly more than a younger swimmer needs. The importance of recovery often is overlooked when training young athletes. Coaches of age group and college teams delight in piling massive amounts of yards on their swimmers. Most can handle the overload because they have the reserve capacity to recover quickly. Those who survive become champions; those who don't try another sport. This shotgun approach to training—do everything and hope something hits the mark—won't work with the older athlete the way it sometimes does for the teenager. The older athlete would not recover from the wounds this approach inflicts. Quitting isn't an option, so learning to rest is essential, to allow extra time for adaptation. Rest doesn't need to be a complete day off. It's not necessary to swim every workout at an exhausting pace. Swimming an entire workout slowly can be more beneficial as recovery than avoiding the pool entirely. It allows the body to recuperate in preparation for the next training stimulus without the mental anguish some people experience when they miss a day of swimming. "At least I got wet!"

Due to an addiction to daily exercise, many lifelong exercisers have a morbid fear of taking a day off from training, as if they would get out of shape if they missed one day of exercise. Physiologically, these fears are unfounded. Although the body loses some of the adaptations of training fairly quickly, 48 hours without exercise is certainly not long enough to detect any changes. Although research has shown daily exercise bouts to be effective in relieving the stress associated with our modern lives, this effect is distinct from that of training to improve performance. Studies have even shown that taking a hot shower is equally effective at improving mood as aerobic exercise or weight training. Rest is good! To that end, the past-50 swimmer would be wise to avoid the pool at least one day a week. If you feel the need to do something physical, less stressful activities such as walking, gardening, or playing with the grandkids are among the many ways to spend Jefferson's "two hours a day on bodily exercise." Then take a hot shower!

Rest has its place *during* a workout, too. Sometimes it takes careful planning, but it's important for the goal of the workout to program rest correctly. Many swimmers over the age of 50 who train seriously share the pool and the workout with much younger, and sometimes faster, swimmers. Unless the workout is planned carefully, this creates difficulties for the slower swimmer. Let's present an example to illustrate this problem, but first we need to review the concepts of interval training presented in chapter 3. We defined two types of interval training according to how much rest is allowed between each repeat. Fast interval training consists of higher quality efforts done with fairly long rest. Slow interval training is characterized by lower quality efforts and short rest. These two types of interval methods challenge the body with distinct training stimuli and elicit distinct physiological adaptations. Yardage mania has promoted the desire to do as many yards as possible in the least amount of time, which motivates the yardage maniac to rest as little as possible during a workout, i.e., slow, short rest interval training. Short rest intervals are valuable in moderation, but it's counterproductive to become obsessed by one form of training to the exclusion of all others. Short rest intervals train the aerobic system, with little benefit to speed development. In order to achieve optimal performance from a training program, however, all the energy systems used in a race must be stressed, not just the aerobic system. The only way to swim fast in a meet is to swim fast in practice.

The following example will illustrate how a well-designed workout set may not have the desired effect for everyone in the pool. Suppose the "young guys" are doing an interval set of 10×50 on 50 seconds. This means they will do 10 repeats of 50 yards leaving every 50 seconds. Wanting to keep up with the young guys, you take up the challenge and attempt to tackle the same set, even though your best time in a meet is much slower than theirs. They are able to comfortably complete the set, averaging between 32 and 35 seconds per 50, whereas you struggle to "make the interval"—finishing each 50 barely before you have to leave on the next one. For the young guys this is a fairly easy short rest set, but for you it is a very *hard* short rest set. The training stimuli are different. You may as well be doing a completely different workout.

Suppose the next part of the workout plan includes another set of 10×50, but this time the send-off interval is one minute, meaning the young guys will get plenty of rest and can average under 30 seconds for each 50. This is considered fast interval training and is beneficial for the development of strength and speed. Again you challenge yourself to stay with the young guys. You get more rest this time, but it's still only about 10 seconds between repeats. You're still doing slow, short rest interval training. You've been cheated out of the opportunity to train for strength and speed, the very qualities the aging body lacks relative to the youngsters. The solution to this problem is to swallow your pride and take more rest. Modify the send-off so you have at least the same amount of rest as the faster swimmers. For example, do the first set of 50s on one minute and the second set on 1:15 or 1:20. In this way, you'll be receiving the same types of training stimuli as the faster

DRURY GALLAGHER

Home: Manhasset, New York
Current age group: 60 to 64
Started Masters swimming at age 34.

As a youngster Drury played basketball, baseball, football, and swam. He was too small for the "ball" sports when he started high school, but he made the swim team because he had tremendous endurance from riding the waves (body surfing) at the beach four to five hours a day as a kid. He improved his speed enough to become an All-American swimmer in high school and college, although he feels he never reached his potential for lack of proper training and coaching. After college he continued to swim, picking up tennis and golf as well, before returning to competitive Masters swimming in 1972.

Courtesy of Drury Gallagher

Drury's most satisfying performances came at the age of 50 when he won six events and set six World Records at the Pan Pacific Games in Indianapolis in "probably my best all around times." He also went six for six at both USMS nationals that year, setting several world and national records in the process. Topping off an exceptional year he went 10 for 10 at a short course meters meet in Florida; 10 events, 10 victories, and 10 World Records in three different strokes!

Drury's workouts range from 2,500 to 5,000 yards depending on his goals, schedule, and time. He has trained under the tutelage of Coach Lisa Baumann for the past decade in a variety of pools without the benefit of a team. This situation has changed with the construction of the Nassau County Aquatic Center on Long Island, originally built for the Goodwill Games in 1998, and the introduction of a Masters program run by Coach Baumann at the new facility. Drury has been handicapped for the past few years by injuries to his neck, right shoulder, and lower back, but rehabilitation is going well and he looks forward to aging up into the 60–64 age group. His goal is to continue swimming until at least the year 2048!

I cannot tell you how important the Masters swim program has been for my overall health and well being. I have been active for the past 25 years and I hope to continue swimming and competing up to the age of 110 (set your goals). It is a tremendous form of therapy.

Drury's Sample Workout

This mid-season workout was written for Drury by his coach, Lisa Baumann, in preparation to swim the 400 IM. The special emphasis of this training session is on his weakest stroke, backstroke.

Warm-up

1 × 300 Free ladder (25 drill-25 swim-50-50-75-75) rest :30

1 × 300 Breast/free ladder (75 kick breast-75 swim free-50-50-25-25) rest :30

8 × 50 Swim

1–4: (25 pull breast w/dolphin kick+25 kick back) on 1:10

5–8: (25 swim back+25 drill fly, right arm/left arm) on 1:00

6 × 125 Swim on 2:00 (Work on stroke tempo & negative splitting each 100 back)

Odds: 25 fly + 100 back

Evens: 100 back + 25 breast

8 × 25 on :40 (recovery)

Odds: underwater breast pullouts (focus: streamline, distance per pullout)

Evens: drill free (fists; catch-up stroke, right arm/left arm, fingertip drag)

4 × 300 Swim on 4:30

1: 100 back + 100 IM + 100 back

2: 100 IM + 100 back + 100 IM

3: Free/back ladder (25 free-25 back-50-50-75-75)

4: Free/back reverse (75 free-75 back-50-50-25-25)

100 easy free drill/swim loosen up

6 × 50 Kick back with Zoomers on :55

4 × 75 Drill (25 fly-25 back-25 breast) on 1:25

4 × 75 Pull free with paddles & buoy on 1:10 (breathe 6-4-2 by 25s, descend #1-4)

6 × 50 Swim IM on :55 (2 × fly/back, 2 × back/breast, 2 × breast/free) (strong turns/stroke conversion, attack the walls)

150 easy choice warm-down

Total: 4,600 yards

swimmers. You also may have to swallow your pride and do fewer repetitions per set, say 9 instead of 10, in order to finish at the same time as the faster group. A well-planned practice session will organize swimmers in lanes by speed, so these modifications aren't a problem. Rest more, do less, but do it well!

There's another issue related to rest that pertains to the construction of a workout. It's not necessary, nor is it productive, to swim every single yard of a workout at top speed. A well-designed workout should include rest sets interspersed between hard sets. This permits active recovery, similar to jogging between hard runs, or soft pedaling after cresting a hill on a bike. Active recovery, as opposed to passive recovery, maintains blood flow to the working muscles so the time it takes to clear metabolic byproducts is decreased. Examples of recovery sets are easy kicking and pulling or stroke drills. With this recovery time built into the workout, the hard sets will be more productive. Easy sets are a great time to socialize, too!

Preventing Injuries

"Prevention is the best medicine." That's easy to say but still true. Since over half of all competitive swimmers will experience shoulder pain sometime in their careers, it's clear where the medicine should be applied. The shoulder exercises presented in chapter 5 are by far the best preventative measures one can take. A strong shoulder will be more stable. Stable shoulders are more likely to be able to withstand the abuse heaped on them by the thousands of repetitions they must make in a year. Let's estimate how many strokes you take in a single 3,000-yard workout. At 20 freestyle strokes per length times 120 lengths of a 25-yard pool you will have taken 2,400 strokes. That's a lot of shoulder flexion and extension, abduction and adduction, internal and external rotation! No wonder shoulder pain is the most common swimming injury.

The chances of an overuse injury are much greater if the correct stroke mechanics are not employed. Biomechanically, the human body isn't well designed to perform many of the movements involved in swimming (the breaststroke kick, for example). In all four strokes the muscles of the upper body are required to generate large forces with the arms above the head. Shoulders aren't designed to withstand these strange movements to the extent to which we subject them. The initial phase of the backstroke pull is an especially awkward motion for the shoulder. Over the years great swimmers have "discovered" the most efficient and least damaging means of performing the strokes by doing what "feels" right to them. We owe these champions a huge debt of gratitude for their motor genius, which has defined the highly evolved competitive strokes we enjoy today. Unfortunately, due to loss of flexibility and strength, the body over 50 years old has a much smaller margin of error in the correct execution of these ideal movements than the pliable 20-year-old body. More attention must be focused on correct stroke technique. Body roll, shoulder rotation, and elbow bend all must be just right to minimize excess stress on joints that aren't prepared to withstand unusual stresses. How can one be sure what is "just right" in stroke mechanics? This is a situation where a trained eye is

Mary E. Messenger

Correct stroke technique can be the best injury prevention.

essential, someone who can critically evaluate stroke mechanics for potentially injury-producing defects—a coach.

The older you are the longer it takes to warm up. You know this from experience, but there's also a sound physiological basis to this statement. Peripheral blood flow decreases with age. This means the joints of the limbs receive less blood and are therefore underlubricated. This is one of the reasons your joints may feel stiff in the morning. Movement of the joint increases blood flow, and the stiffness decreases. It's common sense to commence physical activity very gently, to avoid doing any form of intense effort without warming up thoroughly. Gently swinging the arms in small circles is an excellent way of warming up the shoulder joint before a swim workout,

Gentle arm swings are a good way to start a warm-up.

stretching routine, or resistance training session. Movements can be progressively more forceful as the juices start to flow, so to speak. Every workout should commence with this type of gentle warm-up.

Pain is a very important physiological signal. Pain is the signal that it is time to quit, time to stop doing whatever you're doing that is causing the pain. One of the signs of mild tendinitis is pain at the beginning of the workout that diminishes as the affected area warms up. This stage of tendinitis is usually easy to treat and resolves itself quickly. If not, it's time to stop. The absolute worst thing you can do to an injury is to continue irritating it. Unfortunately, our sport culture has glorified the athlete who toughs it out and "plays through the pain," who keeps going despite an injury. This is a totally unhealthy way to enjoy sports. If it hurts, stop! Of course, this assumes the athlete knows the difference between the pain of an injury and the normal pain associated with intense effort—the "Hurt, Pain, Agony" concept made famous by Doc Counsilman's swimmers in the 1960s. For the past-50 swimmer, it's ridiculous to place pain ahead of pleasure, to aggravate an injury to the extent it prevents enjoyment of the sport. So if a shoulder, an elbow, a knee, or an ankle hurts, get out of the water immediately and begin treating this minor injury so it doesn't grow into a major one.

Treating Injuries

Once you've got a swimming injury, how do you treat it? Many of us are afraid to go to a doctor for treatment because we know what we're going to be told: stop swimming. This is unacceptable advice. Although many people may not consider swimming to be an essential adult activity, you obviously have a different opinion. Fortunately, medical practitioners, many of whom enjoy swimming as a fitness activity as well, have become very understanding of the needs of the serious older athlete. Most doctors today can help you rehabilitate your injury without forcing you to give up all physical activity. Your doctor will start with the least invasive treatment and progress to more drastic measures only if warranted. With persistence most swimming injuries can be resolved noninvasively. Surgery is

International Stock/G.E. Pakenham

Ignoring pain can worsen an injury; if you feel pain, stop swimming and treat your injury.

seldom needed. One of the more recent developments to benefit older athletes is the sport physical therapy clinic. These are clinics that specialize in rehabilitating athletic injuries. They take great pride in successfully returning athletes of all ages to their sports—strong and healthy. So go see a doctor immediately about that small pain and become their next success story.

If you would prefer not to visit a doctor, there are many self-treatment modalities you can use to speed up recovery from an injury. The following list of options assumes that the problem is a sore shoulder, but the basic principles apply to all types of injuries.

1. The most obvious advice is to stop doing the motions that cause pain. This means stop swimming, or lifting weights, or stretching.

2. If swimming freestyle causes pain but breaststroke does not, then swim breaststroke for a while. At least you'll be able to stay in the water.

3. Wear fins during part of the workout to reduce stress on the shoulders.

4. Correct any defects in stroke mechanics.

5. Never use swim paddles if you have delicate shoulders.

6. When performing kicking drills don't extend the injured arm above your head to hold the board. Preferably, kicking should be done without a board, on your side so that the injured arm won't be extended. If you prefer to kick with a board (so you can talk to your friends during the kicking drills) then bend the elbow of the injured shoulder and lay the forearm on the near end of the board as illustrated in (below). The important thing is to avoid kicking with the arm extended above the head.

7. Warm the injured area before exercising. Moist heat is best. For example, wrap the area in a wet towel. Apply ice after exercising for approximately 10 minutes. An ice

Protect an injured left shoulder by bending the elbow during kicking drills.

massage is very effective. The experts use ice cups: paper cups filled with water and placed in the freezer. The paper allows the ice to be held more comfortably while massaging yourself.

8. Consult your doctor about the use of anti-inflammatory medication.

9. Although there is disagreement as to the effectiveness of massage as a means of aiding recovery, it certainly feels good. A trained sports massage therapist may be able to help relax tight muscles surrounding the injured site.

If the injury doesn't resolve itself in a reasonable amount of time, a few days to a week, the only remaining alternative is to seek professional help. It's senseless to limit your activities for weeks, months, or even years due to a chronic injury that could be alleviated with aggressive rehabilitation.

Staying in Shape While Injured

Nothing is more demoralizing than being injured. While you are prevented from following your usual exercise routine, you can feel yourself getting flabby as your conditioning slips away and worry that you'll never be able to get it back. Most past-50 swimmers *hate* taking time off for this reason. What can you do to stay in shape while you are recovering? First of all, being "in shape" means much more than having low body fat. We can identify dozens of physiological changes that take place as a result of endurance and strength training. These changes can be classified as central adaptations that affect the cardiopulmonary system (heart, lungs, and blood) and peripheral adaptations that affect the muscles and capillaries. These adaptations are a function of the type of training you do. However, the heart doesn't know if you are swimming, running, biking, or climbing stairs. It receives signals to pump more blood, so it pumps more blood. The same applies to the lungs. The cardiopulmonary system doesn't care what endurance activity you are performing, the physiological adaptation will be the same. Therefore, even though you cannot swim, you can still keep this system "in shape" by running, walking, biking, rowing, or climbing stairs.

The same can't be said of the peripheral adaptations. Muscle-specific activity is needed to maintain the physiological state attained through training. If you don't continue to use a muscle in its usual way, these adaptations will be lost fairly quickly. We've all seen the muscle atrophy that results when a limb is placed in a cast for an extended period of time. However, there is an interesting physiological phenomenon that gives hope of retaining some of that muscle. In the field of neurophysiology, it's called cross transfer of strength. By exercising the limb on the opposite side of the body, strength loss in the injured limb is lessened. Therefore, if you break your left leg skiing, do resistance exercises with the right leg. When the cast comes off you will have maintained more strength in the left leg than if you had done nothing at all. This phenomenon is a fortunate consequence of the way the nervous system works.

So, even though being injured isn't fun, there is something you can do to maintain conditioning. Any type of endurance activity will serve as exercise for the heart and lungs. Keeping the muscles in shape is more difficult. The best you can hope for is to minimize the loss. It takes hard work, but it is possible to recover from an injury with dedication and persistence. Ginger Ladich Pierson describes how she returned to top form after an injury.

> In 1989 I had rotator cuff surgery with my left arm immobilized for 3 months. My goal was to prove to *myself* that I could do anything if I really wanted it and trained for it. I wanted to take "tops" again at the Pan Pacific Championships in Indianapolis. I won my first event, without having a clue as to what time I would do, in record time. I felt on top of the world.

chapter

7

Realistic Goals for a Past-50 Swimmer

What are reasonable goals for a swimmer over 50 years old? Clearly swim training isn't going to turn back the clock so you're 25 again, but it certainly can make a difference in how you look, feel, and perform. Therefore, realistic goals revolve around physical and emotional health. The past-50 swimmer wants to look good, feel healthy and happy, and perform well. Swimming provides many opportunities to attain these goals. Not so long ago, this wasn't the case. Forty or fifty years ago organized fitness activities for older adults were few and far between. To some extent, serious physical training and competition weren't considered to be appropriate adult behavior. Today the situation is completely different. We're in the golden age of adult sports. Never before have there been so many opportunities to train and compete, nor have there been so many qualified professionals making a living by helping adults reach their exercise goals. What a great time to be adult athletes! Finally we have the opportunity to reach our athletic potential. As the future unfolds it will be interesting to find out what that potential really is.

Many of the swimmers we coach say they don't think of themselves as being over 50 years old. In their minds they see themselves as being much younger, and while in the pool they sometimes act it! These people enjoy swimming, they enjoy exercise, and they enjoy life. The confusion arises when their young minds tell their over-50-year-old bodies to do exercises they may not be prepared to do. This is a case of the mind saying "I can do this," and the body saying "Oh no you can't." It's not that the task is impossible. It probably is an achievable goal, with the proper preparation! Patience is the key, patience to start gently and progress slowly enough to give that over-50-year-old body time to adapt. You can't reach your potential all at once. Pushing yourself too hard too soon is an invitation for injury. However, with the right balance of training and rest the past-50 swimmer can progress physiologically to the point that previously intolerable training loads can be tolerated, much as Doc Counsilman learned while training to swim the English Channel at age 58.

The physical potential of the older athlete is yet to be discovered. The key is to set realistic goals for what your body can withstand during the initial phase of training. Start your program by doing less than you think you are capable of doing, be consistent, and gradually build up to longer, more intense workouts. It may take years of training to reach your potential.

The key to staying motivated over the long haul is to set a realistic goal, attain it, then go after a new, different goal. Your training program always should be designed with a goal in mind. Most people are goal oriented. They use goals as motivation to work hard, whether it be at a job, with their family, or in the pool. Swimming goals are usually individual goals. Best times, or personal records (PRs), are clearly defined goals. Children, and adults who are just learning to swim, improve rapidly and the PRs fall with abandon. It's so fun and exciting that they can't imagine swimming without a PR now and then. Young children are often seen crying when they don't reach their best time at a meet. As the years pass it becomes more and more difficult to improve, and you forget what setting a best time feels like. Rather than cry about it, the adult defines new goals, goals that don't revolve around breaking PRs. Let's look at some goal-setting strategies, ways that you can make swimming fun and exciting for the rest of your life.

Swim Consistently

A good goal for the past-50 fitness or competitive swimmer is to maintain a consistent swimming routine. This type of goal usually consists of a specific distance goal during each training session with a minimum number of days per week in the pool, say one mile a day, five days a week, for example. For optimum benefit a lifelong fitness program must be consistent, so a further goal may be to swim year-round for as long as health permits. How does one stay motivated to keep up this kind of routine for years and years? Obviously the variety of routes available to the fitness runner or cyclist isn't available to the swimmer. Your pool is always going to feature a single black line going from one end to the other. Depending on where you live, however, there may be opportunities to swim in different pools, indoor and outdoor, during the different seasons of the year. Swimming at different times of the day, or modifying distance goals also can add variety. For example, you might try swimming an extra half mile one day a week.

Make Swimming a Social Activity

We all know swimming is an excellent lifelong fitness activity. Swimming with others adds a new dimension, social interaction. Just as runners meet to *go for a run* and bikers *ride together*, swimmers can benefit from group workouts. In order for a long-term exercise program to be effective it must be enjoyable. One of the basic concepts of psychology is that we tend to repeat enjoyable experiences and avoid unpleasant ones. If swimming isn't enjoyable you won't do it, no matter how old you are. Swimming can be very boring when done by yourself—back and forth following a black line. Exercising with other people is a proven means of improving exercise adherence, sticking with it.

Granted, as a social sport, swimming has one big disadvantage. There's less time to talk while swimming than biking or running, in as much as you have your face in the water most of the time. Nevertheless, swimmers share the same sense of camaraderie in the pool that bikers and runners feel on the road or trail. In the pool, however, you don't get left behind! Swimming is a sport where everyone stays together throughout the workout, despite differences in age and skill level. Planned rest breaks between sets let the slower swimmers catch up. Alternatively, the number of repeats can be balanced with the interval time so everyone finishes the set together—the slower people do fewer repeats on a longer interval. Then they all can talk about their shared experience! Although having your face in the water prevents the constant chatter some bikers and runners enjoy about their sport, brief periods of silence can be a blessing to those who are faster of body than of mind. The one or two minutes it takes to do the repeat provides an opportunity to formulate new ideas or responses to the topic of the moment. If you know you'll only have a few seconds between intervals to express your thoughts, you make the words count. Trust us when we say that some very interesting intermittent discussions have been carried out over a long interval set!

Exercise is a great way to loosen up. Have you ever noticed how much easier it is to talk with someone while you're exercising? Have you ever said, "Let's go for a walk" and ended up talking about important career or personal issues? For some reason feelings are easier to share while the body is distracted by physical activity. Sport psychologists claim that exercise relieves stress. Perhaps reduced stress frees us to communicate more openly. Perhaps we are more confident that our deeper thoughts will be more freely accepted and understood by a person with whom we're sharing the sometimes painful physical experience of a workout. Many strong friendships have been forged between the walls of a swimming pool. Whatever the mechanism might be, you can gain both physically and emotionally by sharing fitness activities with other people.

The pool is a great place to meet interesting people, too. Grade school teachers often claim they love their jobs because they are surrounded by great people, the future parents, scientists, educators, doctors, lawyers, and business leaders of our society. The characteristics that will lead these children to successful lives already have been forged. How stimulating it must be for the teacher to associate with such an eclectic group! Over the years, single-minded dedication toward achieving success in a profession can reduce variety in one's life. The people with whom you tend to associate are just like you. They share similar backgrounds, similar lifestyles, similar interests. It's easy to become pigeonholed into a narrow homogeneous niche of the world. By the time they reach middle age many people are ready to break out. Along comes Masters swimming! Where else but in a pool can you meet such a diverse collection of people with completely different backgrounds, professions, and talents? They share a common interest—swimming—which can serve as the springboard for sharing other aspects of their lives. In the water many differences disappear. Everyone is laid bare, with no more than a swimsuit and a pair of goggles as protection. You can't tell someone's occupation by how well they swim. Everyone must go down and back between the lanes. Swimming, the great equalizer! It's so refreshing, such a wonderful change of pace from the rest of your existence, a chance to relax, meet new people you could not have possibly met in any other way, and make new friends.

Swimming is a great way to make new friends.

Besides the social aspect, training with a team can help you become a better swimmer. Although discouraging at times, swimming with someone who is more skilled than you is the best way to improve your own performance. Most experienced swimmers are willing to share their expertise when asked. Much can be learned by simple observation as well, both in terms of underwater stroke technique and workout methods. The process is comparable to learning to write better by reading a Pulitzer-winning author. Group dynamics also play an important role in maximizing the fitness benefits of a training session. The group tends to motivate itself, to spur each individual toward a better effort. You may arrive at the pool totally unmotivated to train, only to get carried along by the group as the workout progresses, so by the end you've had a very enjoyable experience and a tough workout, too. Group dynamics can lead you to make an effort you never would have made on your own. Each member of the team, irrespective of age or speed, contributes to the collective energy of the group. As an older swimmer, it's especially enjoyable to watch the younger members of the team squirm when you show them up, either in performance times or dedication.

Group dynamics also can make setting individual goals easier. When several minds come together, new ideas for swimming adventures are sure to result. Someone suggests a goal, and the rest of the group joins in. The advantage of belonging to a team is that team goals often can motivate you to define individual goals. For example, the team goal might be to have maximum participation in a one-hour timed swim. Swimming all out for an hour straight is certainly not something you would have willingly done on your own! As part of a team function, however, it can be a very enjoyable event, and you're more likely to push yourself to a better performance when your friends are watching. Diverse and challenging team and individual goals add excitement to each new season. Belonging to a good team can make sports as fun as it was when you were a kid!

Learn About Swimming

"If you try to coach yourself you have a fool for a coach." This gem from Doc Counsilman's repertoire of one-liners is testimony to the benefits of training with a team that has a coach. The coach's job is to design the workout, a blessing to those who are intimidated by the complicated training methods described in chapters 3 and 4. After a hard day at the office, it's often refreshing to come to the pool and have someone else tell you what to do. A coach's instruction is also the best way to improve technique. Swimming isn't a sport you can master by reading a book, not even this one!

Thirty years ago, there was no such thing as a Masters swim coach. Older adults who wanted to swim for exercise were on their own. If they were lucky they may have been able to find a sympathetic age group, high school, or college coach who would give them help on stroke technique. Rarely did an adult ever train regularly with a youth team. In those days adults

The assistance of a professional coach can improve your performance and add to your enjoyment of swimming.

were not supposed to take exercise or competition seriously. Fun was for the youngsters only. Today, however, many excellent coaches, Masters swimmers themselves, have chosen to make a living helping adults have fun.

What can a professional coach do for you? It's very difficult to observe yourself swimming, to see what you are doing wrong. Even if you could see yourself, correct stroke mechanics are so complex you probably wouldn't be able to correct your mistakes by yourself. That's where a coach comes into play. He or she has a trained eye to pick out the weaknesses in your technique and help you to correct them. Through the magic of videotape, both above and below the water, you can see everything the coach sees and get immediate feedback. As they say, "a picture is worth a thousand words." When you see what you are doing you'll finally be able to better visualize how to correct the problems you've been told to correct. If you don't have a coach, or don't have access to underwater video equipment, consider attending one of the many clinics held across the country. In sharp contrast to the situation a few years ago, today there are several individuals and organizations dedicated to helping the adult swimmer improve stroke technique. USMS alone offers eight clinics a year that coaches and swimmers can attend. Check the USMS Web site (*www.usms.org*) for current information.

Perform Well

The clock is a great motivator. It never lies! The best way to gauge your swimming performance is to time yourself. For the past-50 swimmer, however, performance is relative. There are only a few individuals who are capable of achieving physical performances equal to, or exceeding, what they could do in their youth. The lucky ones are those who weren't physically active as youngsters. Since they began training late in life there were no previous performance standards with which to compare. These first-time swimmers are in the best possible situation because their performance can continue to improve as better training and technique counteract the physical declines associated with aging. The second-luckiest group consists of people who swam as youngsters, learned the correct stroke mechanics, but didn't compete seriously. They may not have had the economic resources to swim, or maybe a pool was not available, or perhaps they may not have been motivated. By the time they have passed the age of 50, however, most adults have raised a family and are thinking about retirement. Over a lifetime of shouldering the responsibilities of career and family, they are ready to apply the same discipline and motivation to swimming. This group is also capable of performances that exceed what they did as youngsters.

Swimmers who competed seriously in high school or college and have spent a lifetime in the sport, however, must be more realistic about performance goals. Unless they didn't train very seriously as youngsters, very few past-50 swimmers can improve upon their college times. It's just very difficult to invest the same amount of time and energy into a sport as one did while in school. A more reasonable goal at the age of 50 is to perform within 10 percent of those times. Thereafter, judge performance relative to the previous two-year period only, rather than what you did at the age of 22. In this way you can derive satisfaction from doing well within the limits set by your age. You may not be able to do a lifetime best, but you can certainly *perform well.*

There are many ways to gauge swimming performance. The most straightforward way is to see how far you can swim in a given amount of time, say 30 minutes. In swimming jargon this is called a T30 swim. Timed swims are appropriate for all levels of swimming, from the youngest age groupers to the oldest Masters, and can be done about once a month to test endurance. An alternate method is to time yourself over a given distance, similar to the runner who uses the time it takes to run a specific course to monitor fitness. The advantage of the timed swim is that everyone in the group finishes at the same time, regardless of skill level or age. The distance completed is the measure of performance. Thirty years ago, distance swims like these were the only means by which a fitness swimmer could gauge performance. Many people were not satisfied with this approach to fitness swimming and wanted more opportunities to compete. Thus was born Masters swimming, the biggest advancement in adult fitness of the 20th century.

The Masters swimming program was organized in 1970 by Ransom Arthur to offer competitive opportunities for adult swimmers. The first national championships were held that same year in Amarillo, Texas, with 46 participants. The movement grew so rapidly that by May of 1987 more than 2,300 people came to Stanford for the short course national championships! Today, there are tens of thousands of men and women across the country and throughout the world enjoying the benefits of competition in a structured environment. The World Championships, held every two years, draw more than 3,000 people to such diverse places as Japan, Australia, Brazil, Canada, England, and Morocco, in addition to the United States. The national governing body for Masters swimming in the United States is United States Masters Swimming, Inc. (USMS), "an organization of sportswomen and sportsmen . . . dedicated to the premise that the lives of participants will be enhanced through aquatic physical conditioning." Its Mission Statement is "to promote fitness and health in adults by offering and supporting Masters Swimming programs." See the summary below for information on joining United States Masters Swimming. Its Goals and Objectives are stated in the USMS Rule Book are listed on the next page.

HOW TO JOIN
UNITED STATES MASTERS SWIMMING

USMS is open to anyone 19 years of age or older. Membership is administered by the Local Masters Swimming Committee (LMSC), of which there are 55 throughout the country, corresponding roughly to the 50 states. The USMS Web site can be found at www.usms.org, or the national office can be reached at:

> 261 High Range Road
> Londonderry, NH 03053-2616
> (603) 537-0203

Membership fees are currently $15 per year for national expenses plus an additional fee for the LMSC, which in Indiana, for example, is $13. Thus, for a mere $28 per year you can enjoy all the privileges of USMS membership. These privileges include the opportunity to participate in USMS sanctioned meets, secondary accident insurance in all USMS sanctioned events and supervised practices where all participants are USMS registered members, a subscription to *Swim* magazine, and periodic mailings from your LMSC.

GOALS AND OBJECTIVES OF MASTERS SWIMMING

A. To encourage and promote improved fitness and health in adults
B. To offer adults the opportunity to participate in a lifelong fitness and/ or competitive swimming program
C. To encourage organizations and communities to establish and sponsor Masters Swimming programs
D. To enhance fellowship and camaraderie among Masters swimmers
E. To stimulate research in the sociology, psychology, and physiology of Masters Swimming

USMS has been so successful in meeting these goals that they are the models by which all other adult competitive sports are gauged.

The story doesn't end with USMS, however. From its inception, the YMCA has been a leader in promoting aquatic fitness. There are thousands of YMCA pools across the country in which USMS swimmers train. It's really impossible to separate the two programs because so many people belong to both organizations. The YMCA holds its own national meet in April, a couple of weeks before the USMS nationals so swimmers may participate in both meets. Without the YMCA, Masters swimming wouldn't be what it is today.

Why is Masters swimming so popular? Why do grown men and women, many with grandchildren, get so excited about competition in a sport that used to be the domain of kids? Basic human needs have a lot to do with it. As humans we seek such things as love and affection, security, status, challenge, achievement, and recognition. To understand Masters swimming we need to investigate the last three—challenge, achievement, and recognition—more closely. Within each human resides the desire to achieve, to gain a feeling of accomplishment from undertaking a challenging task and completing it. The desire to be recognized for an achievement is natural, especially if the task is difficult. As youngsters, ample opportunities to gain recognition through achievements were available in school, youth activities, and sports. But an adult seldom gets a pat on the back for a job well done. Getting a paycheck is nice, but there are things more valuable than money. Self-satisfaction is one—satisfaction that you have attempted a difficult task and completed it successfully. For some people this is enough. These are the people who are satisfied to work hard at an exercise program solely for the joys of being physically fit. There are others, however, who want more. Fitness as recreation is not enough. They want to compete, to test themselves against others and their own potential. They are motivated by the pressures of competition, and are inspired by others who share their zest for testing themselves.

Adult competitive athletics isn't for everyone. The beauty of Masters swimming is that each individual can choose his or her own level of involvement. Each person is free to choose his or her own form of physical challenge. The recognition that accompanies competitive achievements is valuable to some, while others are satisfied to achieve a personal best time or distance. Either way, basic human needs are being met.

Is competition really necessary? Throughout this book we've stressed the potential of the older athlete, that many of the negative effects associated with aging are actually due to a sedentary lifestyle. Many past-50 swimmers might unleash hidden athletic potential if they push themselves harder, if they train with more intensity. One of the best ways to motivate yourself to train harder is to compete. In general, humans are

SUSAN LIVINGSTON

Home: Marblehead, MA
Current age group: 60 to 64
Started Masters swimming at age 45.

Although Susan grew up in Florida and spent time in the water, she had no formal swim lessons or team competition. At Smith College she was a member of the synchronized swimming and crew teams. Susan was a runner and biker when she started Masters swimming in 1984. She found success almost immediately. Her best performances came at age 47 when she won the national 200-meter backstroke title for the first time. "I had a great coach and was training harder than I ever had. My times have slowed since, due to less coaching and less training (and age?)." Nevertheless, she swam the fastest 200-meter butterfly time in the nation at the 1994 World Championships in Montreal, thereby earning the coveted All-American certificate in the 55–59 age group. Susan "aged up" to the 60–64 age group the day before the 1998 Long Course Nationals in Fort Lauderdale. As the youngest competitor in her age group, she came home with a nice birthday gift of four gold medals. "The best way to turn 60 that I can imagine!"

Susan does three workouts per week, twice with a coach going about 2,600 yards and once on her own. She trains with two or three younger swimmers who do not compete in Masters. Although her dedication to training is not what it once was, she still manages to rank in the National Top Ten list in a number of events.

Trouble with her right arm the past two years forced her to give up weight training, but she hopes to be able to lift weights again. She also walks, bicycles, and occasionally takes classes in tai chi. Here's how Susan feels swimming affects her life:

Courtesy of Susan Livingston

Physically, swimming keeps me feeling fit. It is energizing. I feel fulfilled meeting the challenges of training and competing. Swimming also contributes to my emotional well-being because my achievements boost my self-esteem. I can accept the reality of getting slower as I age and still feel good. There's always the next age group to look forward to! Socially, you cannot beat the camaraderie found in Masters swimming. Whether my own teammates or the friends I have made from other clubs, the people I have met through this activity are an outstanding group.

Susan's Sample Workout

Warm-up: 200 drill swim, 200 kick, 200 pull
Swim 500
    2 × 200 breast
    3 × 100 back
    4 × 50 fly
    Watch the clock and try to keep the same pace on each.
Warm-down 200 breast with fly kick

goal-oriented, competitive beings. That's how we climbed to the top of the food chain. Many people over the age of 50 are now, or have been, engaged in highly competitive occupations. Why do they need more competition? What if they have no desire to go up against the person in the next lane? Although this may sound trite, the beauty of athletic competition for those past the age of 50 is that everyone is a winner. The goal is to improve physical and emotional well-being. Whether you come in first or finish dead last is not the issue. The only losers are those who make no effort to take care of themselves as they age. It isn't necessary to compete in order to take positive steps toward improving your physical fitness. Competitions merely serve as a means by which you motivate yourself to try harder. The competition in Masters swimming isn't against the swimmer in the next lane. It's against yourself, your goals, and the aging process. Don't let old age win!

Types of Competition

As an example of what is available, the USMS national championship schedule is presented in table 7.1. There are many more events at the local level, too numerous to mention here. Competitions can be classified into four categories:

- Traditional meets: These competitions are held in 25-yard, 25-meter, and 50-meter pools with the full complement of events, including relays (single sex and mixed).
- Open water races: Open water races take place in rivers, lakes, and oceans. Expect variable water conditions. Wet suits are not allowed!
- Postal events: Unique to Masters swimming, the postal event is the most convenient way to participate. Swim in your own pool and submit the times by mail to be tabulated. Distances are usually quite long: 5K, 10K, 3,000 yards, etc.
- Fitness events: Fitness events are designed to be noncompetitive and usually involve counting laps completed in a given time. The Hour Swim is an example.

Just as youth swimming is graded into categories by age, Masters swimming is subdivided into age groups by five-year

Table 7.1

ANNUAL USMS NATIONAL CHAMPIONSHIP EVENTS

Month	Event
January	1-Hour Postal Championship
May	Short Course Nationals
May-Sept	5 & 10 K Postal Championship
July	2-Mile Cable Championship
July	1-Mile Open Water Championship
August	2-Mile Open Water Championship
August	Long Course Nationals
Sept-Oct	3,000 & 6,000 Yard Postal Championship
Sept	6+ Mile Open Water Championship
Sept	5K Open Water Championship

© Photophile

Open water swimming can be a great challenge.

increments, for example, 50 to 54, 55 to 59, etc., all the way to 100 and over! Yes, there really are people over 100 who compete! National records are maintained in each age group for three pool lengths: 25 yards (short course), 25 meters (short course meters), and 50 meters (long course). World records are recognized in 25- and 50-meter pools only. One of the best motivators is the yearly National Top Ten Times lists, which are compiled in each event and age group for all three courses. The thrill of seeing your name appear on one of these lists is enough to keep you in the pool year-round. The top swimmer in each event and age group, the *numero uno* in the land, is designated as an All-American and is awarded an appropriately impressive certificate and patch. Isn't competition grand?

It is normal to be intimidated by the competitive aspects of Masters swimming, especially for those who didn't participate in competitive sports as youngsters. Many first-time competitive swimmers think they lack competitive drive and fear the humiliation of being defeated in a race. If they're willing to take the plunge and enter a race, they may be pleasantly surprised. Masters swimmer Susan Livingston describes her awakening like this:

> To this day (thirteen years later) I remember when I discovered I had a competitive streak. Until swim meets, I had never *competed* one on one. In my first New England Championship meet, which was held at Harvard in 1985, I had to race the 100-yard IM (individual medley) against a faster seed. But inspired by a cheering coach and teammate, I went for broke at the sound of the start. It was an incredible feeling to swim hard without letting up. The results were exhilarating: my best time by 1.5 seconds (never again equaled), a New England record for the 45-49 age group, and a decisive win! I discovered the joy of competition that day.

Races are organized in such a way that swimmers are grouped by age and speed so slower swimmers will not be "blown away" by a faster swimmer in the next lane. Nevertheless, competition can be frightening for first-time competitors who are afraid of embarrassing themselves in front of everyone, afraid of being mocked for coming in last or for swimming poorly. Fortunately, it takes only one or two races for this fear to evaporate. Support given by fellow competitors, teammates, and friends reassures competitors that everyone's in the same boat, that everyone who tries is cheered as a winner.

Being able to swim faster or with better technique doesn't make one immune to fear. Even the veterans get nervous before a race. It may be something simple, like will your goggles come off on the dive, or will you start swimming the wrong stroke. (Mistakes happen all the time!) Although they may not admit it, most swimmers are afraid of two things: failure and pain. Fear of failure can take many forms. It may be losing, or performing poorly, or failing to meet a goal time. Fear of pain before a race is a normal reaction to the anticipation of an unpleasant situation. To do well you must leave your comfort zone. Let's face it, all-out efforts hurt! In the longer events fear of failure and fear of pain go hand-in-hand. A failure to concentrate can lead to poor pacing, and a very painful experience at the end of a race. For example, if you swim the

Racing against others your age is a great way to test your fitness.

first half of a 200 fly too fast, the last 50 is going to hurt a lot more than it would have had you paced yourself more wisely.

Many past-50 swimmers don't compete often enough to learn how to overcome these fears. It's hard to learn how to swim a race correctly if it's done in a meet only once or twice a year. Competition teaches you several things. It teaches you how to mentally focus on what you're doing in the water. The shorter events are over so quickly that you don't have time to think. You need to know exactly what you are going to do before the event starts. Swimming in a meet also teaches you how to swim your own race, how to pace yourself based on your best strategy, not the strategy of the person in the next lane. The more often you swim in a meet, the more opportunities you will have to succeed. Each meet lets you know what you'll need to work on before the next meet. So, swim in meets! The more you race, the more you'll learn and the less you'll fear. As Winston Churchill once said, "Success is never final. Failure is never fatal. It's courage that counts."

Racing butterfly requires careful pacing.

One of the best ways to learn an effective race strategy, especially for a race you've never swum before, is to break it into shorter segments in practice. Suppose your goal is to go 3:00 for a 200. That's an average of 1:30 per 100, :45 per 50, or :22.5 per 25. Every time you do race pace or goal set training for 25s, 50s, or 100s in practice try to hit these goal times. If you can do it with long rest one week, try maintaining the same times with less rest the next week. Keep decreasing the rest from week to week while maintaining your goal times, and eventually you'll be able to do the entire 200 straight with no rest at all in under 3:00.

Another method for simulating a race in practice is to do broken swims. A 200, for example, can be broken into 2 × 100, 4 × 50, or 8 × 25. If you take 10 seconds rest between each repeat you'll be able to swim faster than you could if you swam the 200 straight with no rest. Your goal is not to do each 50 in the same time as the one before. In a real race you know the first 50 will be the fastest, and the last 50 is usually the slowest because you're tired. Therefore, if you're doing a broken 200 as 4 × 50 with 10 seconds rest in practice, and you want to hit your meet goal time of 3:00, you'd swim the first 50 a little faster, say 42 seconds. Now you're 3 seconds under your pace. You've got 10 seconds to rest to think about the next 50. Suppose you go :45 on the second 50. You're still 3 seconds under pace. Now you have to do the last 100 in 1:03 to hit 3:00. It's a struggle but you go :46 and :47 on the last two 50s. Bingo! That's three minutes and you've hit your goal time. Coaches say the time you can do on a broken swim with 10 seconds rest after each quarter (50s in this case) is roughly equivalent to what you can do in a meet. It's a real ego booster and confidence builder to achieve your meet goal time in practice, even if the distance was broken into four parts.

Men and women don't race against each other, except in the mixed relays. And, of all the events in a Masters meet, these relays are the most fun. It's exhilarating to watch men and women well past the age of 50 cheering for each other, jumping up and down like a bunch of little kids, enjoying themselves in good competition. Masters swimmer Nancy Ridout explains why she enjoys the mixed relays.

I've always loved to anchor a mixed relay. It's fun to stand up there on the block, getting ready for the last leg. When I glance down the line of my competitors, mostly male, most of whom are "licking their chops" to get in the water and beat this team with a small woman at the end, I get a certain amount of satisfaction knowing I'll hold my own and help my team to victory.

Clearly, there's more to Masters swimming than just winning and losing. In fact, everyone who participates is a winner because they're taking positive action to win the battle against the real foe, growing old.

Triathlon

Before we leave the realm of competition, we need to mention one more opportunity that has become very popular with older athletes in recent years—the triathlon. It's not necessary to add biking and running to your routine in order to enjoy the excitement of this relatively new sport. In addition

Masters swimming is one of the few sports where men and women compete against each other on mixed relays.

You can enter the relay division of a triathlon for a change of pace.

to the individual triathlon, most races also offer a relay division in which the swim, bike, and run segments are completed by three different athletes. Invariably, when someone attempts to form a triathlon relay, a good swimmer is the most difficult person to find. You'll be in great demand for triathlon relays!

The individual races are very exciting, but the relay competitions tend to be less intense, so a first-time participant shouldn't be overwhelmed. Swim distances start at approximately 1,000 meters and rarely exceed 1,500 meters. Wet suits are allowed when the water is cold. Relay teams are not subdivided into as many age groups as the individual races, but relay swimmers start in a separate wave so that they don't have to endure the carnage that typically takes place at the start of a triathlon swim. If you're looking for a change of pace from the pool, an enjoyable day at the beach, give triathlon a try. Sorry, there are no relays at the Ironman in Hawaii!

Performance goals for a triathlete are different than those for a pool swimmer. Because the course length and the conditions of the water vary from race to race, time is not the best indicator of performance as it is in the pool. Instead, focus on how you come out of the water relative to the other people in the race. If you're doing all three segments instead of a relay, then a good goal is to come out of the water feeling strong enough to perform well on the bike and run to follow.

The national governing body for triathlon in the United States is USA Triathlon, headquartered in Colorado. Check their Web site (www.USATriathlon.org) for more information.

Participate

We've discussed consistency, social, and performance goals. Sometimes in life just showing up is good enough. We often hear our past-50 swimmers say they hope they're still swimming when they're 100. How fast they swim won't matter then. When Tom Lane, at the age of 101, swam in the Masters nationals, the entire pool erupted into a standing ovation. They weren't applauding because he won. He was the only person in his age group. They weren't applauding because he did a good time, although it was a world record. No one that age had ever swum in a meet before. They were applauding because he participated! Here's a 101-year-old man doing something that until recently nobody thought was possible for someone his age, competing in a swim meet and loving it! He was truly an inspiration to all the younger people at the meet, which of course was everyone. You could almost hear them making mental notes to themselves. "I'm going to be participating in Masters swimming when I'm that age, too."

You don't need to be 101 to make participation a worthwhile goal. Masters meets, open water swims, and triathlons are held all over the world in some very exotic places. Look through the list of events for any given year and you'll probably find several places you'd like to visit even if there's no race there. Why not use swim meets as an excuse to visit the exotic places you might not visit otherwise? In a case like this, participation is more important than a good performance. You're going on vacation and combining it with a swimming event. What a great way to see the world!

There's one final way to make participation a reasonable goal for the past-50 swimmer. We call it adventure swimming. This is an event that really isn't a competition, although open water racing and triathlon could be considered an adventure for someone who's never done that type of swimming. True adventure swimming involves swimming across, around, or along a body of water. It's not a race. You finish, you win. The challenge is beating the distance and the elements, not another swimmer or the clock. You don't need to swim across the Atlantic or float the length of the Mississippi to find these kinds of challenges. There are plenty of more realistic adventure swimming goals you can set for yourself. Table 7.2 lists a few of them. For more information on open water and triathlon swimming consult Penny Lee Dean's book, *Open Water Swimming*.

Nancy Ridout tells the following story of her first adventure swim:

> The first time I swam the Golden Gate, age 41, the air was cold, it was overcast, and the surf was coming into Ft. Point higher than I am tall. I had never swum in the ocean, the cold Northern California ocean, nor was I an open water aficionado. But I did want to swim the Gate. For me, that was like the English Channel is for others. Finally, after a lengthy period of hesitation and questioning the wisdom of this undertaking, I threw caution to the wind (literally) and ran into the water hoping not to get smashed by the waves. I made it out, was not pushed into the pilings of the bridge (as some were) and

Table 7.2

SELECTED OPEN WATER CHALLENGES

- English Channel, ≈ 21 miles
- Catalina Island Channel, 20.5 miles
- Manhattan Island Marathon Swim, 28.5 miles
- San Francisco Bay, numerous swims of various distances
- Seal Beach, 1, 3, and 10 miles

began my swim. For awhile, a seal accompanied us. We were instructed to come under the bridge about half way, toward the bay side. I was swimming along, looking up at the beautiful Golden Gate Bridge from a vantage I had never before experienced. Life is good. The next time I looked up at the bridge, it was up—but way over there. I was on my way to Alcatraz! I readjusted my course and tried to swim a perpendicular line back to the bridge. It worked! For an up-until-that-time pool swimmer, there was a tremendous amount of satisfaction in the realization that I was a strong enough swimmer to cross the currents, tides, and swells to get back on course.

The benefits, both socially and physically, of participation in an organized swimming program cannot be emphasized enough. There's more to swimming than going fast, than breaking records or winning events. Achieving outstanding perfor-

A positive attitude is an important goal.

mances past the age of 50 takes a tremendous amount of dedication and effort, just as it does at any age. Very few people are willing, or able, to devote the necessary time and energy. When setting goals, you have to be realistic about commitment to exercise, relative to other family and occupational responsibilities. There is, however, an important role to be played by regular, organized physical activity in slowing the aging process. Unfortunately, many swimmers give up the sport when performance declines to what they perceive to be unacceptable levels. It's too discouraging for them to be reminded that they just can't do what they used to do so easily. At this point a change in attitude is necessary, a shift in goals. Swimming slower is better than not swimming at all. The benefits of regular exercise greatly outweigh the disappointment in the inevitable reduction in performance as one ages. So, whenever you're ready, jump in!

chapter
8

A New Age of Swimming: Technology and Techniques

Although swimming is a sport that involves mastery of complex techniques, it isn't a sport that depends on technology. The essentials in swimming equipment, a suit and goggles, have not changed much over the years. Bikers can improve their performance and add variety to their sport by spending large sums of money on the latest bicycle technology. Runners can upgrade to the newest shoe design. Swimming equipment, however, is designed for protection, not performance. Although swimsuit manufacturers can claim that their fabric and design reduce water resistance, your performance is still determined primarily by what's inside your body, not what's on it. Many of the advances in swimming performance in recent years are a result of changes in technique, not technology.

To be sure, the technology of swim training has changed tremendously over the past 30 years. Pools are more comfortable, and there are better tools to make training more effective. Furthermore, modifications to the rules have changed the way

Swim suit designs are constantly evolving.

some of the competitive strokes are being swum. Although none of these changes in technology and technique is unique to the past-50 swimmer, if you haven't been paying attention to the sport for a few years they may take you by surprise. If you're just starting in the sport, then everything we present here will be new to you. To learn more, consult one of the books listed in the references. It's been our observation as coaches that swimmers over 50 are extremely interested in the latest techniques and technology. Because the potential for physical improvement is limited at this age, they go after every little technical edge they can find to take another fraction of a second off their time.

Modern Pools

Everyone over 50 who remembers what swimming pools were like in the 1950s and before has a special appreciation for how much improvement in aquatic facilities has been made since then. First of all, there weren't as many places to swim. You could usually count on a YMCA or YWCA to have a pool, but this was the era before aquatic sexual integration, so men and women did not swim together. Many of these four-lane, 20-yard Y and high school pools were magnificent works of art in marble and tile. Unfortunately, given the technical limitations of the day, they were also often rather dark, and it was difficult to control temperature, humidity, water quality, and air circulation. Conditions could be ideal for training one day and unbearable the next. Many past-50 swimmers have vivid memories of coughing, burning eyes, itching skin, and extremes of temperature.

Thankfully, the situation today is greatly improved. The pools are bigger and more numerous, and their availability to the public has increased. The popularity of swimming as a fitness activity has grown along with the facilities. Most Ys and schools have six- or eight-lane, 25-yard pools, and many large

Modern pools make swimming safe and comfortable.

universities have 50-meter indoor pools. Not only is there much more lane space available for recreation, it's being managed more wisely, with special times set aside for lap swimming. Whereas many of yesterday's pools were pleasing to the eye, today's are pleasing to the eye and the body. Improved water and air quality make them a safe and comfortable environment for regular exercise, resulting in the tremendous growth in swimming as a fitness activity over the past 30 years. This is a great time to be an adult swimmer!

The Latest Tools

Swimming toys. That's what we call the equipment a swimmer uses to train. Most pools today are well stocked with all the necessities for a serious workout: lane lines, pace clocks, kickboards, and pull buoys. Modern flow-through lane lines and large-diameter pace clocks, both Counsilman-inspired

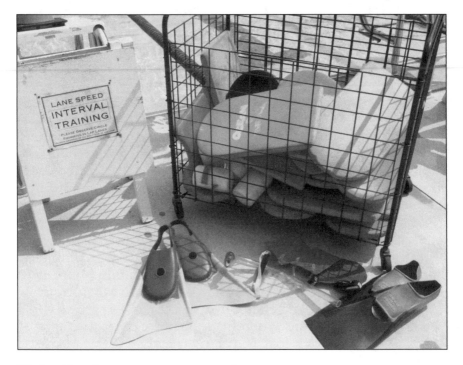

Workout toys!

designs, have changed very little over the years. There have, however, been many attempts to introduce innovative new designs for kickboards and pull buoys, but the original models developed during the '50s and '60s are still the most common design seen on the deck.

The single most important innovation in the past 30 years, the one piece of equipment that has advanced the sport of swimming more than any other, has been the swimming goggle. These gems were introduced around 1969 and immediately changed the workout philosophy of many coaches. Prior to goggles, the workout often was over when the chlorinated water caused so much eye irritation that the swimmers could no longer see. This meant that on days when the water quality was less than ideal the workout could be very short indeed. With the advent of goggles the workout could go on and on. This led to a big increase in the number of yards swimmers were able to train. Dramatic improvements in performance, especially in the distance events, during the late '60s and early '70s, can be attributed in part to the introduction of goggles. They were quite a novelty then. Now no serious swimmer would even think of swimming without them.

Although fins and paddles have been around for many years, their use as training tools has increased in recent years. Wearing fins during a kick set will overload the leg muscles and help build strength. Fins also make kick sets more enjoyable due to the faster speeds one can attain with them. Some past-50 swimmers like to wear fins during a swim set to keep up with the faster swimmers. Fins are also a good way to unload tired arms. Caution! Don't get carried away with fins too soon. Kicking too much or too hard can overstretch the tendons and ligaments of the ankle and result in painful and slow-healing injuries. Paddles also should be used in moderation. They're a great tool for improving stroke technique, but leave the long and hard swim sets with paddles to the younger swimmers. The danger of injuring a shoulder while swimming hard with paddles is too real to merit the risk. Use them to work on stroke technique instead. The smaller the paddle the less stress you'll place on the shoulder, thereby lessening the possibility of injury. A helpful trick for swimming freestyle with paddles is to remove the wrist strap. This forces you to finish the stroke correctly; otherwise the paddle will fall off.

Speed-assisted training, training at velocities greater than can be achieved naturally, is a new technique that is gaining popularity among elite swimmers. It's analogous to running downhill or cycling behind a car. You're able to attain greater speeds than you could without the assist. These supra-speeds teach the neuromuscular system to contract more quickly than normal. The swimmer also learns what it feels like to swim fast, plus it's great fun! Speed-assisted training should be an excellent way for the past-50 swimmer to fire up those fast-twitch muscle fibers. Unfortunately, it takes a lot of time and pool space to do effectively.

Although machines are available to do speed-assisted training (e.g., the Power Reel), a very simple and inexpensive substitute toy is the swim belt. This apparatus consists of an approximately 20-foot length of surgical tubing attached to a web belt that buckles around the waist. The other end is attached to a starting block. The swim belt can be used in two ways. Swimming against the tubing serves as resistance training. Swimming with the tubing is speed-assisted training. The cord is stretched the full length of the pool by pulling on the wall or lane line. The swimmer then pushes off the wall in the best streamlined position possible and swims at full speed,

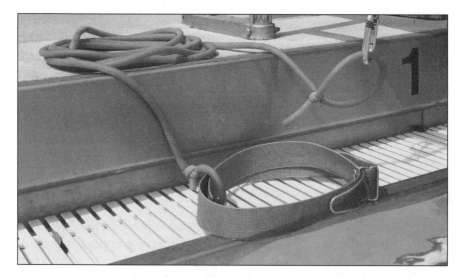

A home-made swim belt tether system.

with the assistance of the tubing. As the tubing goes slack, a coach or helper needs to pull the swimmer the rest of the way to the wall. There are two reasons why this type of training is valuable for the past-50 swimmer. First, it teaches good streamlining, both on the push-off and during the normal stroke. Increased water resistance due to improper body alignment is very noticeable at the higher than normal speeds attained. Second, it stimulates the fast-twitch nerves to fire faster without placing too much stress on the muscles. This is an excellent way to reduce the decline in fast-twitch muscle fibers usually observed as one ages. Speed-assisted training is a technique we expect to see used more often by past-50 swimmers in the future.

Today's Rules

Rules are made to force uniformity, to define the swimming movements so that no one gains an unfair advantage. Over the past 30 years several rules have been changed to conform to innovations in stroke technique, innovations that have made the strokes faster. With minor exceptions, the same rules that apply to elite Olympic swimmers also apply to Masters swimmers. So that all past-50 swimmers can take advantage of recent rule changes, we'll outline them here and discuss how they have affected the way the strokes are swum. You may have to make some technique changes to catch up with what the rules will allow today. The fitness swimmers who do not compete certainly do not need to be concerned about these rule changes. Rules are not an issue for them. But it's been our experience that past-50 swimmers, whether they compete or not, are very interested in learning everything they can about swimming. So, here we go with the new rules!

Freestyle

Freestyle is freestyle—there aren't very many rules. Besides eliminating the requirement that the hand needed to touch the wall on the turn, the only change has been to require that the head break the surface of the water within 15 meters following the dive or push-off. The rule was changed to prevent swimmers from excessive underwater kicking after the start and turns. Some swimmers feel they can kick dolphin underwater faster than they can swim freestyle on the surface. Since most past-50 swimmers aren't interested in kicking the entire length underwater, this rule does not affect freestyle technique.

Breaststroke

The big change in breaststroke, and it is fairly recent, is that your head can go underwater. A quote from the USMS Rule Book is in order: "Some part of the swimmer's head shall break the surface of the water at least once during each complete cycle. . . ." Another change is that the hands may recover *over* the surface of the water following the completion of the arm pull, as long as the elbows stay underwater. These two rule changes opened the door for the further development of a new style of breaststroke swimming called the "wave" breaststroke, which is faster for some swimmers. On turns, the shoulders don't need to remain level while reaching for the wall, making the turn slightly faster. And finally, after a start or turn, you're allowed one underwater pull, one kick, then your "head must

The new breaststroke rules allow the head to go under water during the glide.

break the surface of the water before the hands turn inward at the widest part of the second stroke." Under the old rules you were required to break the surface *before* starting the second stroke. This change makes it faster to get up to swimming speed after a start or turn.

Backstroke

The only recent changes in the backstroke rules involve the start and turn. For meets held in 25- and 50-meter pools, Masters swimming follows the same rules as Olympic swimming, established by FINA (Federation Internationale de Natation Amateur), the international governing body of swimming. Their rules for the backstroke start require that "the swimmer's feet including the toes shall be placed under the surface of the water." For some unknown reason the rule is different for meets held in a 25-*yard* pool, which are not governed by FINA. There are very few 25-yard pools outside the United States, so there's a different set of rules for short course meets in this country. The backstroke start in a 25-yard pool can be done with the toes out of the water, as long as part of each foot is in the water. Standing in or on the gutter, as is often done in high school meets, is not allowed in Masters swimming.

Two changes in the backstroke turn have revolutionized the stroke and drastically dropped record times. You no longer need to touch the wall with your hand and, more importantly, you can turn over onto your stomach and do a freestyle turn. This is the same style of turn that backstrokers have been using in practice for years. The rule is very specific as to how much freestyle you're allowed to swim—after all it *is* a backstroke race. "During the turn the shoulders may turn past the vertical toward the breast, after which a continuous single or a continuous simultaneous double arm pull may be used to initiate the turn. Once the swimmer has left the position on the back, there shall be no kick or arm pull independent of a continuous turning action." You must push off on your back. You still need to look at the backstroke flags to know when to turn over and it's still difficult to judge the turn correctly, but these changes make the new turn several tenths of a second faster than the old turn, and the records have dropped

Many backstroke swimmers benefit from an underwater dolphin kick after the start and each turn.

accordingly. The finish still must be made on the back, plus the backstroke to breaststroke turn in an individual medley race must be done on the back.

The other backstroke rule change was to limit the use of a major innovation in backstroke technique, the dolphin kick. Backstrokers discovered that they could go much faster after the start and turn by doing dolphin kicks underwater. Introduced in the late '70s, this technique was made popular when David Berkoff broke several backstroke world records in the late '80s. It became known as the "Berkoff Blastoff." In a matter of months, swimmers in 50- and 100-yard backstroke races were spending more time dolphin kicking underwater than swimming backstroke on the surface! These events no longer were stroke events but dolphin kicking events. A rule change was imminent. It was decided that the limit would be set at 15 meters after the start and each turn, at which point the head must break the surface.

Butterfly

In 1998 the same rule was passed for butterfly. The head must break the surface within 15 meters of the start and each turn, and any underwater dolphining must be done with the shoulders horizontal, not sideways. Both of these rule changes affect only those backstrokers and butterfliers who are lucky enough to have a dolphin kick good enough to propel them through the water faster than they can swim on the surface. For most past-50 swimmers the rule change isn't an issue. An even more recent change may affect the way some swimmers perform the butterfly turn. As with the breaststroke turn, one shoulder is allowed to drop below the other when approaching the wall. This could speed up the turn slightly.

There is one difference between FINA rules and United States Masters Swimming rules concerning the butterfly kick. Masters swimming allows a breaststroke or whip kick "exclusively or interchangeably with the dolphin kick," while FINA allows only the dolphin kick. This rule gives a real boost to swimmers who have difficulty completing a long butterfly race using the dolphin kick exclusively.

Innovations in Stroke Technique

We have noted that typical past-50 swimmers are very keen to learn everything possible about the latest innovations in stroke technique. They want improved performance, but they are aware of the ceiling in their physical capacity. If brute force won't do it then perhaps finesse will. Improved stroke technique, swimming more efficiently, is a goal that is achievable by swimmers of any age. It's not easy. In fact it's very hard to make technique changes. It takes a lot of patience and a little humility. It takes constant attention and concentration. And it takes a coach or friend who has the time to help you because it's even more difficult to change your technique by yourself.

A word of warning is in order. Just as bike gadgets come and go and running shoes go out of style, some technical innovations in swimming do not withstand the test of time. A swimmer breaks the world record using a unique style, and everyone immediately tries to copy it. Who's to say the swimmer didn't break the world record despite his or her technique? The stroke modification may be unique to that individual, beneficial to him or her but harmful to someone else. Valuable innovations will outlive the originator and be adopted by the majority of swimmers in the years to come. Others will fade with time, just like any fad. The grab start, the wave breaststroke, the underwater dolphin kick, and streamlining are examples of innovations that have withstood the test of time and are now standard techniques.

An example of the life cycle of a technical innovation is being played out in the world of elite swimming. For the last 100 years the freestyle hand entry has been done with the thumb and index finger first, palm facing outward. Based on the technique of one Olympic champion, a few coaches and TV analysts claim that the correct hand entry should be with the little finger first, palm facing inward. Not only does this technique contradict a hundred years of tradition, scores of world records, and millions of swimmers, it is biomechanically difficult to do and violates common sense fluid dynamics. We shall see if this technique withstands the test of time. Therefore, our word of warning to you is the following. Read and listen with a critical mind, then observe the better swimmers in the pool. If an innovation seems reasonable, try it. If it works for you, adopt it. If it doesn't seem reasonable to you, then let it fade away.

Streamlining

Across strokes, there currently is a huge emphasis on streamlining the body after the starts and turns, and even during the stroke itself. It's no longer acceptable to push off like Superman, with the arms at shoulder width. If you push off like a barge, you'll swim like one! The correct streamlined position is illustrated in the photo on page 153. The form is almost identical for all four strokes: head squeezed tightly between the upper arms, shoulders hunched, arms straight, one hand on top of the other, feet pointed, body as straight and narrow as possible. You'll never be moving faster in the water than you are after the start and each turn, so you want to take advantage of that speed by presenting as little resistance to the water as possible. The streamlined position should be held until you feel like you are slowing down enough to make taking a stroke necessary. Hold the glide too long and you'll be starting dead in the water. Start pulling too soon and you'll scrub off speed

Streamlining to reduce drag is a valuable technique in all four strokes.

by destroying the streamline. Knowing when to make the transition from glide to stroke comes with practice.

Maintaining a streamlined position while you swim is not as easy to "feel." Every time you pull with your arms, breathe, kick, or roll your body in the water you disturb the ideal streamlined position. The key is to do these movements in such a way as to create the least amount of resistance to forward motion. One of the best ways to feel an unnecessary increase in resistance caused by a stroke defect is to be dragged through the water while you swim, as with the speed-assisted training described above. Poor streamlining will be obvious because you'll feel the water pressure against the protruding body part.

Many coaches have argued that the body creates less resistance to forward movement underwater if the shoulders are vertical as opposed to horizontal—the body is on its side as opposed to prone. In a pioneer study to test this hypothesis, Doc Counsilman performed a simple experiment. By dragging a swimmer underwater at various speeds he could measure the resistance of the body in different positions. The swimmer created the least resistance when dragged in the prone position. Slightly greater resistance was measured at all speeds when the swimmer was dragged in the side position. Being rolled by an external force while being dragged created more resistance, and the highest resistance of all was measured when the swimmer introduced the roll himself by moving the arms and legs. This study was done more than 30 years ago and should be replicated with today's technology before we can resolve the question of ideal body position underwater. What Counsilman measured was *passive* drag. The swimmers were passively holding a streamlined position while they were being pulled through the water. We need to measure *active* drag, the resistance created as the swimmer performs the complete stroke. Techniques are available for making these measurements. We're anxiously waiting for someone to do the study. In any case, we know that streamlining and body position are important. We also know that *natural* fluid body roll is necessary for efficient stroke mechanics. Counsilman's study would suggest that trying to force body roll increases resistance and slows you down.

CAROLYN FERRIS BOAK

Home: The Woodlands, Texas
Current age group: 50 to 54
Started Masters swimming at age 32.

Carolyn was a six-time national finalist as a teenager, swimming her best times at age 17. She picked up Masters swimming at the age of 32 and at 37 swam long course times comparable to those she did at age 17. Three years later, at age 40, she swam her life-time bests at the short course nationals in Brown Deer, Wisconsin, setting three national records in the process. Her record in the 200 IM, a lifetime best, stood for eight years. She gains satisfaction not in breaking records, however, but in close competition against the best swimmers, people such as Ardeth Mueller and Diana Todd.

Courtesy of Carolyn Boak

Carolyn trains four to six days per week, with a coach. She lifts weights one or two times per week for 30 minutes, but doesn't enjoy it. Lately she's been running two or three times per week instead of swimming.

When I feel grouchy and go swimming I feel mellow afterward. The most important effect of Masters swimming was I met my husband, Tom, through Masters. My volunteer efforts as meet director and committee person are more important than the swim records. My proudest accomplishment was being meet director of the largest USMS Nationals ever—Stanford 1987.

Carolyn's Sample Workout (for IM)

Warm-up: 400

8 × 50 kick (2 each stroke)

8 × 50 drill down, swim build back (2 each stroke)

4 × 400 IM

   1 straight on 7:00 or 7:30

   1 break 10 sec each 100

   1 break 10 sec each 50

   1 break 10 sec each 25

   Working on increasing speed to 200-yard pace

10 × 50 descend

Warm down: 200–300

Body Roll

Much has been written recently about the importance of body role in freestyle and backstroke, as if this were a revelation in stroke mechanics. Actually there's nothing new about body roll. In 1968, after years of careful study, Doc Counsilman wrote the following about body roll in freestyle.

The total amount of roll in degrees, as approximated from observing underwater movies, varies among good swimmers from 70° to 100°. It is wrong to try to hold either the shoulders, the hips, or both in a flat position. It is also wrong to roll just to be rolling. When correctly exploited, the roll serves several purposes:

1. Makes the recovery of the arm easier and permits a shorter radius of rotation of the recovering arm

2. Places the strongest part of the arm pull more directly under the center of gravity of the body

3. Places the hips in such a position that the feet can thrust at least partly sideward during the kick, thus canceling the distorting effect of the recovering arm

4. Facilitates breathing

Doc's swimmers rolled between 35 degrees and 50 degrees to either side! Freestylers today are not rolling any more than they did 30 years ago. Even the great Johnny Weissmuller, the progenitor of the American crawl, rolled his shoulders when he swam, despite the claim in his 1930 book that his "effort is to keep the shoulders 'flat,' never dipping one shoulder down into the water, as this would destroy my hydroplaning position and cause resistance on such a dipped shoulder." Great swimmers often do what *feels* right, as opposed to what they've been told to do, or even what they think they are doing. Watch Weissmuller swim in an old Tarzan movie and see how much he rolls! No, there's nothing new about body roll.

In recent years, a good deal of attention has been focused on the role of hip rotation as a source of power for the arm movements of the freestyle and backstroke pulls. An analogy has been made with the importance of hip rotation in the swing of a golf club or a baseball bat. Anyone who has played golf knows how important it is to get a firm grip on the ground with your feet. That's what the little spikes on the bottom of golf shoes are supposed to do. The feet have a good solid object, the earth, against which to push so that the hip rotator muscles can generate the large force needed to send a drive 300 yards down the fairway. In biomechanics this is called a closed chain system. Swimming is an open chain activity. The feet are not firmly planted upon a solid object. The hip rotator muscles cannot generate large forces because the feet have nothing against which to push, other than the water. Hip rotation can't generate propulsion in swimming, an open chain sport, like it can in golf, a closed chain sport. In freestyle and backstroke, one of the functions of the kick is to balance the movements of the arms. Rotation of the hips and shoulders is a means of transferring forces between the arms and legs, a natural consequence of the balance between pull and kick.

Distance per Stroke

We have two final comments about freestyle technique, two methods of maximizing propulsion that have been around for many years but may be new to some swimmers. The first is Distance Per Stroke (DPS), meaning that the goal in freestyle, and all the other strokes as well, is to cover the maximum distance possible with each stroke. Since it's difficult to measure distance traveled in water with one stroke, a count is taken of the number of strokes required to cover a fixed distance, say one length of the pool. This number is then referred to as your "stroke count." The goal then becomes to reduce your stroke count, to take as few strokes as possible per length. This is done by concentrating on obtaining the maximum propulsion from each pull. Instead of taking short choppy strokes, strive for long, smooth pulls. The most common mistake made by older swimmers is to cut the end of the stroke short, to finish the pull too soon. The hand should continue pulling past the bottom of the swimsuit as the triceps extend the arm. This is the portion of the stroke during which elite swimmers generate the greatest forces. In fact, the speed at which the hands are moving during the final third of the pull is one of the main distinguishing factors between fast swimmers and slow swimmers. Slower swimmers have much less hand speed. Therefore they generate less force and achieve less distance with each stroke. Unfortunately, finishing the pull correctly requires more effort, so when you are tired (or just being a little lazy) you tend not to do it. It takes concentration. Think distance per stroke, DPS, and eventually the proper pull will become a habit.

Our second tip concerns getting the maximum distance from the first stroke after a turn. This tip takes concentration, too. Everyone's first priority after being submerged following the turn is to come up for air. The most expedient way to do that would be to take a breath on the first stroke. Resist the temptation! If you normally breathe on the right side, start your first pull with the left arm. If you plan to take your first breath on the left side, then start your first pull with the right arm. This method forces you to take one arm stroke before you take your first breath, keeping you in a more streamlined position for a fraction of a second longer. It also prevents that stop-dead-in-the-water phenomenon caused by breathing on the first stroke following the turn. You'll still get plenty of air, but you will be moving forward when you get it.

Breaststroke

Breaststroke technique varies so much from individual to individual that it's difficult to say what is correct and what is not. The classical, fairly flat style is probably still the most popular among past-50 swimmers. It's the style that most people learned first and find most comfortable. The newer so-called "wave" breaststroke, which originated in the 1970s, is more difficult to master. The differences between the two styles are apparent from above the water, whereas the underwater movements are similar. The shoulders rise higher for the breath and the head goes underwater following the breath in the wave style. The recovery of the arms is very fast, and some swimmers bring their hands out of the water as they push forward. The goal is to minimize resistance and achieve a more streamlined position during the kicking phase. The assistance of an experienced wave breaststroker may be needed to master

The wave breaststroke can be difficult to learn.

this new style. We recommend that past-50 swimmers perfect the classical style before attempting the wave breaststroke. The new style isn't necessarily faster for everyone. Some people can learn to do it and others can't. If you're satisfied with the classic style don't attempt to change.

Backstroke

The biggest innovation in backstroke, and possibly the entire sport of swimming, has been the introduction of the underwater dolphin technique following the start and turns. It takes practice. The most successful way to do it is to stay about three feet underwater, maintain a streamlined position, and perform small, fast dolphin kicks as opposed to large, slow kicks. The trick to keeping water from coming up your nose is to blow air out the entire time you are underwater. Clearly this technique isn't appropriate for everyone, but it's worth trying in practice to see if it works for you.

There are quite a few older swimmers who prefer the double arm backstroke to the conventional backstroke crawl. This is perfectly legal. The rules state only that you must remain on your back throughout the race. In double arm backstroke, the

Many past 50-swimmers prefer the double arm backstroke.

arms perform the conventional backstroke pull pattern simultaneously instead of alternating. It is difficult, if not impossible, to achieve the optimal bend in the elbows using the double arm technique because the symmetrical arm action does not permit body roll. The legs can do the conventional back flutter kick or a breaststroke kick, as with elementary backstroke. Don't be afraid to try this stroke in a meet if it suits you. World records have been set using it!

Butterfly

The underwater dolphin technique is catching on in the shorter butterfly races too. The technique is the same as backstroke except that you are face down, and the shoulders must remain horizontal. Although butterfly has a reputation for being the most tiring of the four strokes, it's surprisingly popular with the older age groups. There's always the option of switching to a breaststroke kick when tired, which makes it a little easier to get the arms out of the water on the recovery. Some past-50 butterfliers have found it helpful to de-emphasize the final third of the arm pull, that last little push with the triceps that we stressed as being so crucial for getting the maximum distance per stroke on freestyle. Proponents of this modification of traditional butterfly stroke mechanics claim that they tire less and can maintain a faster turnover rate during the longer butterfly races. It must work for them because world records have been broken using this technique.

Starts

A wonderful feature of Masters swimming competitions is that those who are not comfortable diving from a starting block are permitted, and encouraged, to start from within the water. The proper technique involves one hand on the wall, the other arm pointing toward the other end of the pool, and both feet planted together on the wall with the toes pointed to the side. It makes no difference which hand is on the wall, right or left, but most people prefer to face the starter. When the starting signal sounds, let go of the wall and swing the arm over the water to meet the other arm underwater, push off below the water's surface, and streamline. You will lose a few seconds by not diving, but at least you'll be in the water safely, and your goggles won't fall off.

Around 1970 a new start was introduced that made all others obsolete. It's called the grab start because the swimmer grabs the front of the starting platform with the hands. The grab start is an improvement over the conventional arm swing start for two reasons: 1) by using the arms to pull down, the center of gravity of the body can be lowered more quickly; and 2) by pushing against the front of the block the arms can be thrown forward with more momentum. The result is that a correctly executed grab start gets a swimmer off the block and into the water faster than an arm swing start, although the latter start has the advantage of gaining added distance and should be used on relays. Properly instructed, a healthy swimmer of any age can perform this start effectively. The sequence is as follows:

1. At least one foot must be at the front of the block.
2. When the starter says "Take your mark," lean forward and gently grab the front of the block. The hands may be either inside the feet or outside the feet. Keep the thumbs in front, not on top, of the block and do not grab too

You may start a race from within the water if you wish.

tightly. Shift your body weight as far forward on the feet as possible without falling into the water. Hold this position, motionless, until the start.

3. At the start signal (gun or horn), pull down with the arms to lower the body, then push against the front of the block to throw the arms straight forward.

4. Push off the platform with the legs.

A modification of the grab start is the track start, so named because the swimmer places one foot behind the other in the manner of a track sprinter. The action of the arms is the same as with the grab start. Whether or not the grab start or the track start is faster seems to depend on the individual and the degree to which one style has been practiced over the other. Experiment with both and choose the one that works best for you.

In Johnny Weissmuller's fascinating book, *Swimming the American Crawl*, there is a sequence of pictures illustrating the "shallow plunge" popular in the 1920s. He describes it like this: "To get my stroke going as quickly as possible after hitting the water, I make a shallow plunge. I make a tremendous

Two types of racing start: Grab start on the left, track start on the right.

splash with the arms and legs in order to prevent a deep plunge which will delay the start of my stroke." No one plunges (dives) like this today! Not only is it painful to land flat on the water, but the surface tension that must be overcome decreases forward velocity. The goal now is to enter the water through as small of a hole as possible to minimize the effect of surface tension and maximize streamlining. The result is that the angle of attack as the body enters the water is steeper than it was in Weissmuller's era. The best way to learn how to dive through a smaller hole is to practice in a diving well or pool at least two meters deep. By experimenting with the head held slightly lower (a necessity for diving with goggles on) and the legs slightly higher, the optimal angle can be mastered. The trick to diving through a small hole without going too deep (an obvious danger in a shallow pool) is to arch the back slightly immediately after the upper body enters the water.

There has been one more innovation in starting techniques that has become popular in recent years. It involves relay starts. The rules state that "the team of a swimmer whose feet have lost touch with the starting platform (ground, deck, or

Diving through a small hole results in a clean entry.

wall) before the preceding teammate touches the wall shall be disqualified." This means that the second swimmer on a relay can do anything he or she wishes as long as his or her feet are still touching the starting platform when the first swimmer touches the wall. Until recently this meant the last three swimmers on a relay used the conventional arm swing start, timing the swing so that the feet left the block precisely at the moment the previous swimmer touched the wall with the hand. Then some bright person had an idea. Why not take a running start? It's within the rules. Sure, timing the run-up is tricky, but the forward momentum gained makes it worth the risk. This relay start is becoming more popular in Masters competitions, but practice it several times before you get to the meet!

Stroke Drills

Stroke drills are an application of the part-whole method of teaching—perfect each part of a complex task, then combine the parts into a whole. For example, because there are so many things to think about when you swim, it can be much easier to concentrate on doing a movement correctly with just one arm at a time. Drills are effective if the skills learned by themselves transfer to the whole stroke. They're a waste of time and effort if this transfer doesn't take place. Although stroke drills can be a valuable learning tool, dedication to them should not be so obsessive that you miss the enjoyment of swimming the whole stroke. A few of the more popular stroke drills are described in table 8.1. A more complete collection, 91 different drills, can be found in *Swimming Drills for Every Stroke* by Ruben Guzman.

Table 8.1

SELECTED STROKE DRILLS

Freestyle

- One arm freestyle—Swim with one arm only, holding the other arm in front for stability. Allows concentration on one arm movement only.

- Catch-up freestyle—Alternate arms but only one stroke at a time. Wait for the previous stroke to "catch up" before starting the next. Hands touch in front of the head. Allows concentration on one arm at a time.

- Fingertip drag—Swim normal freestyle but drag the fingertips across the surface of the water, with the elbow raised, during the recovery. Teaches the high-elbow recovery.

Breaststroke

- Long glide breaststroke—Hold the glide as long as possible after each stroke. Promotes efficient kick, pull, and streamlining.

- Kick with arms at side—Kick without a board, arms at the side. Bring the legs up far enough on the recovery so that the finger tips touch the heels. Promotes complete recovery of legs in preparation for the kick.

- Inverted kicking—Kick on your back, arms above your head. The knees should break the surface of the water. Promotes proper flexion of the hips.

Backstroke

- One arm backstroke—Swim with one arm only. The other arm can be above the head or at the side. Allows concentration on one arm only.

- Double arm backstroke—Both arms together. Touch the back of the hands together on the recovery, arms straight. Promotes straight arm recovery and balanced arm pulls.

- Pull on the lane lines—Swim close enough to the lane line so that you can pull on it from underneath. The idea is to force yourself to bend the elbow 90°.

Butterfly

- One-arm butterfly—Swim with one arm only, dolphin kick, breathe forward. Allows concentration on one arm only.

- Left arm, right arm, full stroke—Cycle through one, two, or three strokes with one arm, then the other, then both. Breathe during the full stroke only. Promotes body undulation and proper timing of kick with pull and breathing.

chapter

9

Sample Workouts

Throughout this book we've emphasized the importance of structure in the design of a training program. The sample workouts in this chapter illustrate the principles discussed previously and can be used as a guide for designing your own plan. They're divided into two seasons, or macrocycles, winter and summer. Each season is divided into distinct phases, or mesocycles, each with a specific training emphasis. A sample week, or microcycle, is given for each mesocycle. The workouts within a microcycle should be performed in the order presented to properly periodize stress and recovery. The overall goal for each workout is stated, as is the specific purpose behind each set. The winter and summer workouts reflect two distinct styles because they were written by different coaches, each with his own philosophy of training. There's no unique secret formula, no perfect training plan that guarantees success. There are many ways to achieve the same effect, as long as the basic principles are applied correctly.

Although these workouts were performed by Masters swimmers of all ages, no special modifications were made to accommodate those over 50 years old. As we've mentioned before, skill level is a better determinant of performance than age. Distances and rest intervals were established by the capabilities of the average swimmer in the group. Some of these workouts are very challenging. Like performance, the difficulty of a workout is dependent upon fitness level, not age. It's possible, then, that some teenage swimmers will find them too difficult to complete, while some 60-year-olds will find them not sufficiently challenging. The rest between repeats and the number of repeats should be modified to suit the requirements of each individual swimmer. Although workouts are written for six or seven days of the microcycle, most swimmers typically take a day or two off, attending four or five workouts per week. Unless otherwise stated, the stroke to be swum in a given set is at the discretion of each individual, as is the use of paddles and fins. Although a cooldown is not always written into the workout, it's understood that one is included in the conclusion, the distance being at the discretion of each individual swimmer.

Workouts for a Winter Macrocycle

The following set of winter workouts were performed by the Indiana University Masters Swim Team. Practices were held in a 25-yard pool, from 11 a.m. to noon. Although it sounds complicated, a season's plan for a winter macrocycle is fairly simple, consisting of two mesocycles, preparation and competition. General preparation takes place from September through November, specific preparation in December and January, precompetition in February, main competition in March and April, and taper in late April to early May for the Nationals in mid-May. The transition mesocycle from winter to summer seasons is usually no more than a few days out of the pool to recuperate.

Microcycle in the General Preparatory Mesocycle

These seven workouts were done in November and represent a microcycle in the general preparatory mesocycle of the winter macrocycle. The emphasis of the training is on aerobic development, stroke technique, a few sprints, and individual medley (IM) sets using all four strokes. The emphasis of each workout illustrates the stress-recovery pattern of a periodized microcycle: aerobic, maintenance, aerobic, maintenance, aerobic, recovery, aerobic.

Monday

Aerobic Base
Emphasize controlled pace on the main set
Total distance: 3,100

General warm-up
Warm-up 200 swim, 200 kick, 200 pull, 200 swim
Specific warm-up
Swim 4 × 100 on 1:45
Main set
Swim 4 × {200 on 3:15, 100 on 1:45, 50 easy}
Each 100 slower
Descend the 200s *(each 200 faster)* and ascend the 100s
Conclusion
Swim 10 × 50 on 1:00 alternate one kick and one pull

Tuesday

Maintenance
Emphasize kicking and strokes
Total distance: 3,000

General warm-up
Warm-up 800 any way you wish
Specific warm-up
Swim 4 × 50 on 1:00 strokes, kick 4 × 50 on 1:00
Main sets
Swim 300 two strokes
Kick 4 × 50 on 1:00, swim 4 × 50 on 1:00 strokes
Swim 200 two strokes
Kick 4 × 50 on 1:00, swim 4 × 50 on 1:00 strokes
Swim 100 IM
Kick 4 × 50 on 1:00, swim 4 × 50 on 1:00 strokes
Conclusion
Swim 200 easy

Wednesday

Aerobic Base
This is a special birthday workout*
Total distance: 3,100

General warm-up
Warm-up 850
Main set
Swim 45 × 50 on :45 Birthday Set

*It is the custom in this club to swim a special set on one's birthday. For the older swimmers this consists of repeating 50s, the number and interval being equal to the age of the birthday swimmer. In this case it was the 45th birthday of a team member. Therefore, there is an advantage to growing older—more rest between repeats!

Thursday

Maintenance
Moderate pace, with lots of kicking and pulling
Total distance: 3,000

General warm-up
Warm-up 800
Specific warm-up
Kick 4 × 50 on 1:00, swim 4 × 50 on :45
Main sets
Swim 400, kick 4 × 50 on 1:00, pull 4 × 50 on :50
Swim 2 × 200 on 3:00, kick 4 × 50 on 1:00, pull 4 × 50 on :50
Swim 4 × 100 on 1:30, Kick 4 × 50 on 1:00, pull 4 × 50 on :50
Conclusion
Kick 4 × 50 on 1:00

Friday

Aerobic Base
Emphasize the main set—a descending ladder
Total distance: 3,500

General warm-up
Warm-up 800 any way you wish

Specific warm-up
Pull 10 × 50 on :50
Main set
Swim 500 on 7:30, 400 on 6:00, 300 on 4:30, 200 on 3:00, 100 on 1:30 *(Increase speed on each rung of the ladder)*
Conclusion
Kick 10 × 50 on 1:00
Swim 200 easy

Saturday

Recovery
Day off

Sunday

Aerobic Base
This workout is of moderate intensity
Total distance: 3,200

General warm-up
Warm-up 200 swim, 200 kick, 200 pull, 200 IM
Specific warm-up
Swim 8 × 50 on :45
Main sets
Swim 3 × 200 on 3:30 descend
Swim 3 × {4 × 100 on 2:00 fly/back/breast Pac-Man Set*}
Do one set of 4 × 100 of fly, back, and breast
Conclusion
Swim 200 easy

*Here's how a 4 × 100 Pac-Man set works: 1st 100 do 25 stroke/75 free, 2nd 100 do 50 stroke/50 free, 3rd 100 do 75 stroke/25 free, 4th 100 do all stroke. Therefore, the stroke "eats up" the free.

Microcycle for the Specific Preparatory Mesocycle

The next seven workouts were done in January and represent a microcycle in the specific preparatory mesocycle of the winter macrocycle. The emphasis has shifted more toward power, high-quality efforts, more sprints, but without abandoning the aerobic base. The microcycle pattern is: aerobic, maintenance, power, maintenance, aerobic, power, recovery.

Monday

Aerobic Base
This workout has some high-quality efforts
Total distance: 3,200

General warm-up
Warm-up 800
Main sets
Swim 2 × {5 × 100 on 1:45} *(Hold a steady pace on each set of 5; switch strokes on 2nd set if you wish.)*
Swim 2 × {2 × 200 on 3:15, 2 × 100 on 1:45} *(First one of each set of 2 hard, second easy)*
Conclusion
Swim 200 easy

Tuesday

Maintenance
Only the 4 × 100 should be hard—lots of kicking
Total distance: 3,000

General warm-up
Warm-up 800
Specific warm-up
Kick 4 × 50 on 1:00
Main sets
Swim 2 × 200 on 3:00
Kick 4 × 50 on 1:00
Swim 4 × 100 on 1:50 *(Hold fast pace.)*
Kick 4 × 50 on 1:00
Swim 8 × 50 on :50 descend 1 to 4 and 5 to 8 *(4th and 8th 50s should be fast)*
Kick 4 × 50 on 1:00
Conclusion
Swim 200 easy

Wednesday

Power
> The broken 200s should be near race pace
> Total distance: 3,200

General warm-up
> Warm-up 800

Main sets
> Swim 4 × 50 stretch on stroke *(distance per stroke)*
> Swim 5 × {200 broken on 3:00, 200 easy on 3:30} Broken
> 200s: rest 20 sec after 100, 10 sec after 150

Conclusion
> Kick 200

Thursday

Maintenance
> Recovery from yesterday
> Total distance: 3,100

General warm-up
> Warm-up 900

Main set
> Swim 300 on 4:15, 2 × 150 on 2:00 or 2:15, 4 × 75 on
> 1:15
> Kick 300

Conclusion
> Swim 5 × {4 × 50 IM order} on 1:00

Friday

Aerobic Base
> Challenge yourself to make the short intervals
> Total distance: 3,400

General warm-up
> Warm-up 200

Specific warm-up
> Swim 8 × 100 on 1:40

Main sets
   Swim 4 3 100 on 1:25
   Swim 6 3 100 on 1:40
   Swim 3 3 100 on 1:20
   Swim 4 3 100 on 1:40
   Swim 2 3 100 on 1:15
   Swim 5 3 100 on 1:25

Saturday

Power
   Emphasize the hard 100s, 50s, and 25s
   Total distance: 3,100

General warm-up
   Warm-up 800
Specific warm-up
   Kick 8 × 50 on 1:00
Main set
   Swim 4 × {100 moderate, rest 10 sec, 100 hard, rest 20 sec, 50 moderate, rest 10 sec, 50 hard, 50 easy}
Conclusion
   Swim 10 × 50 on 1:00 (25 easy, 25 hard)

Sunday

Day Off
   Recovery

Microcycles in the Competitive Mesocycle

The following workouts represent three microcycles of the main competition mesocycle in March leading up to the state meet. The team rested a few days to peak for the state meet, then did a full taper for the national meet in May. The first two seven-day microcycles emphasize power, while the last emphasizes maintenance in preparation for the state meet. Note that there's much more high-quality swimming in these microcycles than there was during the preparatory microcycles described above. This example illustrates the essence of periodization. The characteristics of the workout are determined by the phase (preparatory or competition) of the training cycle.

Monday

Recovery
Day off

Tuesday

Power
The important features are the two sets of hard 50s
Total distance: 3,200

General warm-up
Warm-up 500 swim, 200 kick
Specific warm-up
Swim 10 × 50 on 1:00
Main sets*
Swim 200 easy
Swim 4 × 50 on 1:15 hard
Swim 200 easy
Swim 4 × 50 on 1:15 (25 easy, 25 hard)
Swim 200 easy
Kick 4 × {75 on 1:30 moderate, 25 on :30 all out} *(This kick set allows recovery of the arms before the next swim set.)*
Swim 4 × 100 on 2:00 descend *(The last one should be very hard.)*
Conclusion
Swim 200 easy

*The sets of 50s are hard efforts, to develop speed; the 200 easy swim is for recovery.

Wednesday

Maintenance
Easy day to recover from power workout on Tuesday
Swim 2,000 easy any way you wish

Thursday

Power
> Another day of hard efforts
> Total distance: 3,200

General warm-up
> Warm-up 200 swim, 200 kick, 200 pull, 200 swim

Specific warm-up
> Swim 16 × 50 on :45
> Swim 4 × 200 on 3:15 one easy, one hard
> Kick 200 easy
> Kick 4 × 50 on 1:15 hard
> Swim 16 × 25 alternating one slow one fast, start fast one every 1:30

Friday

Maintenance
> Allows recovery from the two previous days of sprinting
> Total distance: 3,000

General warm-up
> Warm-up 500 swim

Main sets
> Swim 4 × 100 IM on 2:00
> Swim 100 easy
> Swim 8 × 50 IM order on 1:00
> Swim 100 easy
> Swim 2 × 200 IM on 3:30
> Swim 100 easy
> Kick 200 IM easy
> Swim 2 × {200 on 3:15, 100 on 1:30, 50 on 1:00, 2 × 25 on :30} *(Moderate effort)*

Saturday

Aerobic Base
Work on strokes; descend sets so that last repeat is hard
Total distance: 3,500

General warm-up
Warm-up 200 swim, 200 kick, 200 pull, 200 swim
Specific warm-up
Swim 8 × 50 on :50 or 1:00 warm-up set
Main sets
Swim 2 × {4 × 100 on 2:00 descend} stroke
Kick 200 easy
Kick 4 × 50 on 1:15
Swim 5 × 200 on 3:00 or 3:15 or 3:30 descend
Conclusion
Swim 100 easy warm down

Sunday

Recovery
Day off

Monday

Power
Hard efforts on 100s, 50s, and 25s make this a power workout
Total distance: 3,000

General warm-up
Warm-up 200 swim, 200 kick, 200 pull, 200 swim
Specific warm-up
Swim 8 × 50 on :45
Kick 1 × 100 on 1:45, 2 × 50 on 1:00, 2 × 25 on :45
Main sets
Swim 400 moderate
Swim 4 × 100 on 2:00 hard
Swim 200 moderate
Swim 4 × 50 on 1:15 hard
Swim 12 × 25 one easy one hard, start fast 25s on 1:30
Conclusion
Swim 50 easy warm-down

Tuesday

Maintenance
Recovery from yesterday's sprint workout
Total distance: 2,900

General warm-up
Warm-up 600
Specific warm-up
Kick 200 easy
Kick 2 × 50 on 1:00
Main sets
Swim 20 × 50 on :50 moderate
Swim 4 × 200 on 3:15 descend *(Moderate effort)*
Conclusion
Swim 200 easy

Wednesday

Aerobic Base
This is a low-quality aerobic base workout
Total distance: 3,200

General warm-up
Warm-up 800
Specific warm-up
Kick 200, kick 4 × 50 on 1:00
Swim 6 × 50 on :45
Main sets
Swim 400 moderately hard
Swim 2 × 200 on 3:30, first one recovery, second one hard
Kick 100 easy, Kick 2 × 50 on 1:00
Swim 5 × 100 on 1:20 or 1:30, just make the interval
Conclusion
Swim 8 × 25 every other one fast, start the fast 25s on 1:30

Thursday

Specific Speed

The main set is a goal set: very hard!
Total distance: 2,200–2,500

General warm-up
Warm-up 600
Specific warm-up
Kick 2 × 100 on 1:45
Kick 2 × {75 moderate on 1:30, 25 hard on :45}
Swim 6 × 50 on :45
Swim 200 moderate
Main set
Swim 3 × 100 on 5:00 or 3 × 200 on 8:00 *(These are all out efforts—repeated time trials.)*
Conslusion
Swim 400 easy

Friday

Maintenance

Recovery from Thursday's goal set
Total distance: 3,200

General warm-up
Warm-up 200 swim, 200 kick, 200 pull, 200 swim
Specific warm-up
Swim 6 × 50 on 1:00 down stroke/back free
Kick 2 × {75 moderate on 1:30, 25 hard on :45}
Kick 4 × 25 on :45
Main sets*
Swim 300 moderate
Swim 4 × 50 on 1:15 descend
Swim 300 moderate
Swim 3 × 100 on 2:00 descend to 90 percent
Swim 300 moderate
Conclusion
Swim 2 × 200 on 3:30 *(First one accelerate (each 50 faster), second one decelerate (each 50 slower).*

* The main set is moderate; only four hard efforts: last 50 of 4 × 50, last 100 of 3 × 100, last 50 of the first 200, and first 50 of the last 200

Saturday

Recovery
Day off

Sunday

Aerobic Base
Work on controlled, steady pace
Total distance: 3,200

General warm-up
Warm-up 800 any way you wish
Specific warm-up
Kick 2 × 100 on 2:00, 2 × 50 on 1:00, 2 × 25 on :45
Main sets
Swim 200 easy
Swim 5 × 100 on 1:45 moderate—hold steady pace
Swim 200 easy
Swim 5 × 100 on 1:45 controlled, just to the point of discomfort
Swim 200 easy
Conclusion
Swim 12 × 25 one easy, one hard, start fast 25s on 1:30
Swim 150 easy

Monday

Maintenance
This is a moderate workout to allow recovery
Total distance: 3,000

General warm-up
Warm-up 200 swim, 200 kick, 200 pull, 200 swim
Specific warm-up
Kick 4 × 50 on 1:00, 2 × 25 on :45
Swim 8 × 50 on :50
Main set
Swim 3 × {200 on 3:00, 100 on 2:00, 50 on 1:00, 50 easy}
Conclusion
Swim 6 × 50 one hard, one easy, start fast 50s on 2:00
Swim 50 easy

Tuesday

Maintenance

Easy workout to prepare for the meet on Saturday
Total distance: 2,050

General warm-up
Warm-up 150 swim, 150 kick, 150 pull, 150 swim
Specific warm-up
Swim 4 × 50 on :50
Kick 75 on 1:30, 50 on 1:00, 25
Main sets
Swim 2 × 100 on 1:15, 1:20, or 1:25 *(Controlled, steady pace)*
Swim 100 mental practice for event *(This is not an all-out effort but should be at a controlled pace to mentally rehearse your event.)*
Swim 300 easy
Swim 3 × 50 on 1:00 *(Controlled, steady pace)*
Swim 50 mental practice for event *(Rehearse your event.)*
Conclusion
Swim 300 easy
Practice starts and turns

Wednesday

Maintenance

Swim smoothly without working too hard
Total distance: 1,800–2,000

General warm-up
Warm-up 150 swim, 150 kick, 150 pull, 150 swim
Specific warm-up
Swim 6 × 50 on 1:00 descend 1 to 3 and 4 to 6
Swim 100 easy
Main set
Swim 3 ×100 on 2:00 descend or 5 × 100 on 1:20 or 1:30 steady pace *(Those swimming distance events on Saturday go 5 × 100)*
Swim 100 easy
Kick 200 easy, kick 2 × 25 on :45

Conclusion
  Swim 4 × 25 on :45 build-up each 25 to full speed
  Swim 50 easy

Thursday

Recovery
  Day off or swim 2,000 easy

Friday

Maintenance
  Practice warm-up for the meet on Saturday
  Total distance: 1,500–2,000

Warm-up
  Warm up as you will before the meet
Main sets
  Swim 5 × 50 on 1:00 smoothly and crisply
  Practice starts, turns, and streamlining
  Swim 5 × 50 on 1:00 hold steady pace
Conclusion
  Warm down

Workouts for a Summer Macrocycle

The transition mesocycle between winter and summer seasons is usually fairly short, consisting of a few days of total rest. During the summer macrocycle it's advantageous to train in a long course 50-meter pool, if one is available, since the meets are held in pools of that size. The first few workouts in the longer pool should be done at very low intensity. The transition from short to long course is very stressful on the shoulders because there are fewer turns. Even though you might not stop at the wall, performing the turn requires different muscles, which gives the swimming muscles a brief rest.

The following set of long course workouts were performed by the Indy SwimFit Masters team. Although written by a different coach, the basic components of workout structure are present: general warm-up, specific warm-up, main sets, and conclusion. These workouts were designed to be done in a 50-meter pool, but they are perfectly adaptable to short course pools, either yards or meters. The only factor that needs to be considered when switching workouts from meters to yards is that a meter is about 10 percent longer than a yard, so times will be about 10 percent slower as well. Rest intervals should be adjusted accordingly.

Practices were held at 5:15 a.m. on the weekdays and 7:30 a.m. on Saturdays in the months of June, July, and August. Because the summer macrocycle is so much shorter than the winter macrocycle, the preparatory and competitive mesocycles are much shorter as well. General preparation takes place in late May, specific preparation in June, precompetition in early July, main competition in late July and early August, and taper in mid-August for the Nationals in late August. The transition mesocycle follows in early September and corresponds to the switch back to a short course pool, unless the weather is good and the outdoor pool stays open later into the fall. If not, this transition mesocycle is a wonderful time to give swimming a rest and enjoy other outdoor activities.

Microcycle in the Preparatory Mesocycle

This set of six workouts corresponds to the preparatory phase of the summer season during the month of June. The emphasis is on distance, stroke drills, and IM.

Monday

Aerobic
  Emphasize distance
  Total distance: 4,000

General warm-up
  Warm-up 400

Main sets
  Swim 4 × 150 on 3:00, first all free, second/third/fourth
  last 50 stroke
  Swim 4 × 500 broken on 9:00 *(This is a hard aerobic set.)*
      First: 400 easy/moderate, rest :50, 100 good effort
      Second: 300 easy/moderate, rest :40, 2 × 100 rest
      :05 good effort
      Third: 200 easy/moderate, rest :30, 3 × 100 rest :05
      good effort
      Fourth: 100 easy/moderate, rest :20, 4 × 100 rest
      :05 good effort
  Swim 12 × 50 on 1:10, alternate drill/stroke by 50s
Conclusion
  Kick 400 no fins, choice of stroke

Tuesday

Maintenance
  Strokes and IM
  Total distance: 3,800

General warm-up
  Warm-up 400
Main sets
  Kick 8 × 50 on 1:05, IM order
  Swim 8 × 50 on 1:05, alternate drill/backstroke
  Swim 5 × 100 on 1:55 back, descend 1–5
  Swim 6 × 150 on 3:00 IM
      First and fourth: fly/back/breast by 50s
      Second and fifth: fly/back/back by 50s
      Third and sixth: fly/breast/breast by 50s
  Swim 8 × 50 on 1:10, choice of stroke, descend 1–8
  Pull 400 free, alternate sides on breathing
Conclusion
  Kick 400 easy, IM order

Wednesday

Aerobic
Middle distance
Total distance: 3,600

General warm-up
Warm-up 400
Main sets
Swim 4 × 100 on 2:00, breath control every 3rd and 5th stroke by 50
Swim 16 × 150 on 3:00 free, good effort *(This is a hard aerobic set)*
Distance/Triathletes: do all 150s
Middle distance: sit out every 5th 150
Sprinters: sit out every 3rd 150
Conclusion
Kick 400 easy, reverse IM order

Thursday

Aerobic
Middle distance
Total distance: 3,800

General warm-up
Warm-up 400
Main sets
Kick 200 on 4:15, choice of stroke
Swim 4 × 700, rest 1:00 *(#2 and #3 are broken swims)*
First: Moderate pace, negative split
Second: 2 × 350 negative split, rest :35
Third: 7 × 100 hold pace, rest :10
Fourth: Straight, faster than 1st
Conclusion
Kick 400 easy, worst stroke

Friday

Maintenance
  Strokes and IM
  Total distance: 3,900

General warm-up
  Warm-up 400
Main sets
  Kick 4 × 100 on 2:10 IM
  Swim 6 × 50 on :55 IM order
  Swim 2,400 free and IM as follows: (fast on free, easy on
  IM, or vice versa)
      500 free, rest :45, 4 × 125 IM, rest :15
      400 free, rest :45, 4 × 100 IM, rest :15
      300 free, rest :45, 4 × 75 IM, rest :15
      Negative split free, descend IM
      IMs are fly/back/breast, back/breast/free, etc.
Conclusion
  Swim 400 easy

Saturday

Power
  This workout is very challenging!
  Total distance: 4,600

General warm-up
  Warm-up 400
Main sets
  Swim 6 × 50 on 1:05 back/breast/free by 25s
  Swim 10 × 50 on 1:00 drill/stroke by 25s, choice of
  stroke
  Swim 12 × 150 in 3 sets of 4 *(This is an aerobic set to
  warm up for goal set.)*
      First set of 4 rest :20
      Second set of 4 rest :15
      Third set of 4 rest :10
  Kick 8 × 100 on 2:00, two of each stroke
  Swim 4 × 100 on 4:00 free, good effort! *(This is Goal Set
  training!)*

Conclusion
Swim 400 easy

Sunday

Recovery
Day off

Microcycle in the Precompetition Mesocycle

This set of five workouts corresponds to the precompetition mesocycle in the middle of July. The emphasis has shifted toward more speed, some sprints, and strokes other than freestyle.

Monday

Aerobic
Middle distance
Total distance: 3,900

General Warm-up
Warm-up 400
Main sets
Swim 6 × 100 on 2:00 free, alternate breathing every 3rd/5th stroke by 25
Swim 3 × 200 on 4:00 free, descend 1–3
Swim 400 free in a time double 3rd 200 of previous set
Pull 3 × 200 on 4:00 free, descend 1–3
Pull 400 free in a time double 3rd 200 of previous set
Kick 3 × 100 on 2:10, choice of stroke
Kick 200 in a time double 3rd 100 of previous set
Conclusion
Swim 400 easy

Tuesday

Maintenance
Emphasize fly and kicking)
Total distance: 3,250

General warm-up
Warm-up 400

Main sets
    Swim 300 on 6:30 free/stroke by 25s
    Kick 3 × 100 on 2:20 fly with fins
    Kick 3 × 100 on 2:10 free with fins
    Swim 10 × 25 on :40 fly with fins
    Kick 2 × 200 on 4:40 with fins, fly on 1st, free on 2nd
    Swim 10 × 50 on 1:00, choice of stroke
    Kick 2 × 200 on 4:40 with fins, free on 1st, fly on 2nd
Conclusion
    Swim 400 easy

Wednesday

Power
    Emphasize strokes
    Total distance: 3,000

General warm-up
    Warm-up 400
Main sets
    Swim 16 × 25 on :45 drill, 4 of each stroke
    Kick 8 × 50 on 1:10 alternate breast/fly
    Swim 8 × 50 on 1:00 alternate breast/fly
    Swim 4 × 100 on 2:00 free as 75 moderate and 25 sprint!
    Swim 3 × 100 on 2:00 free as 50 moderate and 50 sprint!
    Swim 2 × 100 on 2:00 free as 25 moderate and 75 sprint!
    Swim 1 × 100 on 2:00 free sprint for time
Conslusion
    Swim or Kick 400 easy

Thursday

Maintenance
    Emphasize distance and strokes
    Total distance: 3,600

General warm-up
    Warm-up 400

Main sets
  Kick 400 reverse IM
  Swim 8 × 50 on 1:00 choice of stroke
  Swim 5 × 400 on 8:00 as 300 free, rest :30, 100 stroke
Conclusion
  Swim 400 easy

Friday

Power
  Broken swims to learn race pace*
  Total distance: 2,000

General warm-up
  Warm-up 400
Main sets
  Swim/Kick/Pull/Swim 800 by 200s
  Swim 200 Broken at 50 with :10 rest, 95% effort, then
  swim 200 easy
  Swim 100 Broken at 50 with :10 rest, 95% effort, then
  swim 100 easy
Conclusion
  Swim 200 easy

*These broken swims simulate a meet effort. By breaking the race into parts you can
concentrate on how fast you need to swim on each 50 to achieve your goal time.
Use broken swims to learn race pacing and build confidence in your abilities

Saturday

Recovery
  Day off

Sunday

Recovery
  Day off

Microcycles in the Main Competition Mesocycle

This set of 14 workouts corresponds to two microcycles in the main competition mesocycle during late July and early August. The emphasis is on preparing to compete, therefore there's more high-quality swimming. These workouts don't constitute a true taper, although they do allow a couple days of rest in order to peak for the weekend meets. A true taper, as for the Nationals later in August, would be as long as two weeks and would allow much more rest.

Monday

Maintenance
Work on pacing
Total distance: 3,150

General warm-up
Warm-up 400
Main sets
Swim 4 × 50 on 1:05, easy with perfect stroke
Swim 300 on 6:00, stroke/free drills by 50s
Swim 4 × 50 on 1:10 easy, stroke other than free
Swim 3 × 100 on 1:50, free, steady even pace, 80 percent effort
Swim 3 × 50 on 1:10 easy, stroke other than free
Swim 3 × 100 on 1:45, free, steady even pace, 80 percent effort
Swim 3 × 50 on 1:10 easy, stroke other than free
Swim 3 × 100 on 1:40, free, steady even pace, 80 percent effort
Swim 3 × 50 on 1:10 easy, stroke other than free
Swim 3 × 100 on 2:00, free, faster pace than above, 95 percent effort
Conclusion
Kick 400 easy, alternate swim/kick, choice of stroke

Tuesday

Maintenance
Work on swimming smoothly with good technique
Total distance: 3,000

General warm-up
Warm-up 800, 50 hard/50 easy on 2nd 400
Main sets
Swim 16 × 50 on 1:10, choice of stroke
Swim 4 × 100 on 2:00, drill/swim by 25, choice of stroke
Swim 200 with good form and 90 percent effort, choice of stroke
Conclusion
Kick 400 choice of stroke
Pull 400 free, alternate sides on breathing

Wednesday

Aerobic
Broken swims to learn race pace
Total distance: 2,000

General warm-up
Warm-up 400
Main sets
Swim 200 on 3:30 free, moderate pace
Kick 200 on 4:00 choice of stroke
Pull 200 on 3:30 free, alternate sides on breathing
Swim 2 × 400 broken on 10:00, rest :10 after each 100, free, 95 percent effort
Conclusion
Swim 200 easy

Thursday

Maintenance
Broken swims to learn race pace
Total distance: 1,800

General warm-up
Warm-up 400

Main sets
Swim/Kick/Pull/Swim 800 by 200s, choice of stroke
Swim 200 broken at 50 with :10 rest, 95 percent effort
Conclusion
Swim 400 easy

Friday

Maintenance
Easy workout on the day before the meet
Total distance: 2,100

General warm-up
Warm-up 400
Main sets
Swim 1,000 free, moderate pace
Kick 5 × 100 on 2:00, choice of stroke
Conclusion
Swim 200 easy

Saturday

Power
Hoosier State Games meet

Sunday

Power
Hoosier State Games meet

Monday

Maintenance
Broken swim to maintain feeling of swimming fast
Total distance: 1,900

General warm-up
Warm-up 400

Main sets
  Swim 300 on 5:00 free, moderate pace
  Kick 300 on 6:00 choice of stroke
  Pull 300 on 5:00 free, moderate pace
  Swim 2 × 100 broken on 5:00, rest :10 after 50, stroke, 90 percent effort
Conclusion
  Swim 400 easy

Tuesday

Power
  Sprint 25s and 50s
  Total distance: 2,800

General warm-up
  Warm-up 400
Main sets
  Swim/Kick/Pull/Swim 800 by 200s, free
  Swim 4 × 25 on :40, stroke, hard/easy, easy/hard
  Swim 4 × 25 on :50, stroke, take only 3 breaths
  Swim 4 × 25 on :40, choice of stroke
  Swim 4 × 50 on 3:00, use same stroke for each, 95 percent effort
  Pull 300 on 4:30, alternate sides on breathing
  Kick 8 × 50 on 1:05, choice of stroke
Conclusion
  Swim 400 warm-down

Wednesday

Maintenance
  Swim the 100s smoothly with good form, not all out
  Total distance: 1,900

General warm-up
  Warm-up 400

Main sets
  Kick 4 × 50 on 1:00, choice of stroke
  Pull 200 on 3:00, free
  Swim 8 × 25 on :30, hard/easy, easy/hard, 2 of each
  stroke
  Swim 5 × 100 on 6:00, choice of stroke, good effort
Conclusion
  Pull 400 free, alternate sides on breathing

Thursday

Power
  Practice your 100 race pace on the set of 5 × 50 on 4:00
  Total distance: 1,650

General warm-up
  Warm-up 400
Main sets
  Kick 4 × 50 on 1:00, choice of stroke
  Pull 200 on 3:00, free
  Swim 8 × 25 on :30, hard/easy, easy/hard, 2 of each
  stroke
  Swim 5 × 50 on 4:00, choice of stroke, good effort
Conclusion
  Pull 400 free, alternate sides on breathing

Friday

Maintenance
  Warm-up workout for the meet on the weekend
  Total distance: 1,800

General warrm-up
  Warm-up 400
Main sets
  Swim/Kick/Pull/Swim 800 by 200s, choice of stroke
  Swim 200 broken at 50 with :10 rest, 95 percent effort
Conclusion
  Swim 400 easy

Saturday

Power
Lakeside meet

Sunday

Power
Lakeside meet

More Workouts!

It's not easy designing your own workouts. That's why coaches have a job. If you are like most past-50 swimmers, you don't have a coach. For more training ideas you can consult *The Fit Swimmer: 120 Workouts & Training Tips* by Marianne Brems. Want even more? Thanks to the wonders of modern technology there's an almost unlimited supply of workouts through the Internet. Not only does the USMS Web site (www.usms.org) post sample workouts, but links are available to Masters teams throughout the country. Many of them post their daily workouts! In this way you can enjoy the benefits of following a training program written by a professional coach for as long as you choose to continue swimming, which we hope will be a long, long time.

Bibliography

Chapter 1

Shea, E.J. 1986. *Swimming for seniors*. Champaign, IL: Leisure Press.

Chapter 2

Costill, D.I. 1987. The physiology of aging in relation to swimming. In *American Swimming Coaches Association World Clinic Yearbook*. Fort Lauderdale, FL: American Swimming Coaches Association.

Dummer, G.M, P. Vaccaro, and D.H. Clarke. 1985. Muscular strength and flexibility of two female masters swimmers in the eighth decade of life. *Journal of Orthopaedic and Sports Physical Therapy* 6(4):235-237.

Rahe, R.H. and R.J. Arthur. 1975. Swim performance decrement over middle life. *Medicine and Science in Sports* 7(1):53-58.

Richardson, A.B. and J.W. Miller. 1991. Swimming and the older athlete. *Clinics in Sports Medicine* 10(2):301-318.

Shephard, R.J. 1997. *Aging, physical activity, and health*. Champaign, IL: Human Kinetics.

Spirduso, W.W. 1995. *Physical dimensions of aging*. Champaign, IL: Human Kinetics.

Stager, J.M., L. Cordain, and T.J. Becker. 1984. Relationship of body composition to swimming performance in female swimmers. *Journal of Swimming Research* 1(1):21-26.

Swan, P.D. and D.L. Spitler. 1989. Cardiac dimensions and physical profile of masters level swimmers. *Journal of Sports Medicine and Physical Fitness* 29(1):97-103.

Trappe, S.W., D.L. Costill, M.D. Vukovich, J. Jones, and T. Melham. 1996. Aging among elite distance runners: a 22-yr longitudinal study. *Journal of Applied Physiology* 80(1):285-290.

Vaccaro, P., G.M. Dummer, and D.H. Clarke. 1981. Physiological characteristics of female swimmers. *The Physician and Sportsmedicine* 9(12):75-78.

Vaccaro, P., S.M. Ostrove, L. Vandervelden, A.H. Goldfarb, D.H. Clarke, and G.M. Dummer. 1984. Body composition and physiological responses of masters female swimmers 20 to 70 years of age. *Research Quarterly for Exercise and Sport* 55(3):278-284.

Whitten, P. 1992. Just how much do we decline with age? *Swim* 8(4):17-20.

WTIU/30 Indiana University Television. 1980. *Doc: The oldest man in the sea.* (video) Bloomington, IN: Indiana University.

Chapter 3

Colwin, C.M. 1992. *Swimming into the 21st century.* Champaign, IL: Human Kinetics.

Costill, D.L., E.W. Maglischo, and A.B. Richardson. 1992. *Swimming.* Oxford: Blackwell Scientific Publications.

Counsilman, J.E. and B.E. Counsilman. 1994. *The new science of swimming.* Englewood Cliffs, NJ: Prentice Hall.

Maglischo, E.W. 1993. *Swimming even faster.* Mountain View, CA: Mayfield.

Selye, H. 1956. *The stress of life.* New York: McGraw-Hill

Chapter 4

Bompa, T.O. 1999. *Theory and methodology of training.* Champaign, IL: Human Kinetics.

Haverland, B. and T. Saunders. 1995. *Swimmers guide: Directory of pools for fitness swimmers.* Stuart, FL: ALSA.

Weissmuller, J. 1930. *Swimming the American crawl.* London: Putnam.

Chapter 5

Anderson, B. 1980. *Stretching.* Bolinas, CA: Shelter Publications.

Aronen, J. 1985. Swimmer's shoulder. *Swimming World* 26(4): 43-47.

Wharton, J. and P. Wharton. (1996) *The Whartons' Stretch Book.* New York: Times Books, Random House.

Chapter 6

Counsilman, J.E. and B.E. Counsilman. 1994. *The new science of swimming.* Englewood Cliffs, NJ: Prentice Hall.

Chapter 7

Dean, P.L. 1998. *Open water swimming.* Champaign, IL: Human Kinetics.

United States Masters Swimming. 1998. *United States Masters Swimming 1998 rule book.* Londonderry, NH: USMS.

Chapter 8

Ballatore, R., W. Miller, and B. O'Connor. 1990. *Swimming and aquatics today.* St. Paul, MN: West.

Counsilman, J.E. 1968. *The science of swimming.* Englewood Cliffs, NJ: Prentice Hall.

Counsilman, J.E. 1977. *The complete book of swimming.* New York: Atheneum.

Counsilman, J.E. and B.E. Counsilman. 1994. *The new science of swimming.* Englewood Cliffs, NJ: Prentice Hall.

Davies, S. and J. Harrison. 1992. *Learn to swim in a weekend.* New York: Alfred A. Knopf.

Guzman, R.J. 1998. *Swimming drills for every stroke.* Champaign, IL: Human Kinetics.

Katz, J. 1996. *The all-American aquatic handbook: Your passport to lifetime fitness.* Boston: Allyn & Bacon.

Katz, J. and N.P. Bruning. 1993. *Swimming for total fitness: A progressive aerobic program.* New York: Doubleday.

Laughlin, T. 1996. *Total immersion: The revolutionary way to swim better, faster, and easier.* New York: Simon & Schuster.

Maglischo, E.W. 1993. *Swimming even faster.* Mountain View, CA: Mayfield.

Schubert, M. 1996. *Competitive swimming: Techniques for champions.* Lanham, MD: Sports Illustrated Books (Time).

Tarpinian, S. 1996. *The essential swimmer.* New York: Lyons & Burford.

Thomas, D.G. 1990. *Advanced swimming: Steps to success.* Champaign, IL: Human Kinetics.

Thomas, D.G. 1996. *Swimming: Steps to success.* Champaign, IL: Human Kinetics.

United States Masters Swimming. 1998. *United States Masters Swimming 1998 rule book.* Londonderry, NH: USMS.

Weissmuller, J. 1930. *Swimming the American crawl.* London: Putnam.

Whitten, P. 1994. *The complete book of swimming.* New York: Random House.

Chapter 9

Brems, M. 1984. *The fit swimmer: 120 workouts & training tips.* Chicago, IL: Contemporary Books.

Index

About the Authors

Mel Goldstein and **Dave Tanner** are accomplished swimmers, coaches, and writers. Both men swam under Doc Counsilman, the legendary swim coach whose Indiana University teams won six NCAA National Championships. These two Counsilman disciples took different career paths but reconnect on this project, allowing them to share their passion for and expertise in Masters swimming.

Goldstein is a past president of United States Masters Swimmers. He is an elite swimmer, ranked in the United States Masters Top 10 in his age group in several strokes. He won the 400-meter IM at the 1994 World Masters Swimming Championships at age 55. Goldstein has also been a Masters swim coach since 1983. He developed and is the swim coach/director of the YMCA Indy SwimFit Program for YMCA of greater Indianapolis. This program has more than 250 swimmers who either compete in Masters swimming and/or triathlons competitively or have chosen aquatics as their activity for physical fitness. Mel and his wife Judy live in Indianapolis.

Tanner brings in-depth knowledge of Masters swimming from three perspectives: as a competitor, coach, and researcher. He's been swimming competitively since 1958 and coaching at various levels from beginner to elite since 1973. He currently coaches at the high school level. An exercise physiologist, his graduate work at Indiana University included human performance research in Masters swimming. Tanner is also active in ultra-endurance sports and is the only person to complete the Hawaii Ironman Triathlon, the Western States 100-Mile Endurance Run, the Race Across America (RAAM), and the Manhattan Island Marathon Swim. He lives in Bloomington, Indiana.